CAUTION!

This book is so filled with joyful wisdom
it is about to explode into a burst of laughing light!

This book will lighten you up in the sense of illuminating your inner path to happy freedom. As you ponder and apply what you read here, you will see with increasing clarity:

- ✓ Your worry produces the conditions you worry about, and you can stop it.

- ✓ Releasing yourself from troubling thought brings the trouble-free life you truly want, and you can do that.

- ✓ You can instantly exit any situation that you do not want and enter freedom.

- ✓ Waiting for things to change before you accept happiness keeps you in unhappy chains, and you can stop doing that.

- ✓ Nothing and no one stands in your way.

Tools of the Tree
Atlanta, Georgia USA

ISBN-10 0-9628666-3-6
ISBN-13 978-0-9628666-3-0
Copyright information available upon request.

First Printing, 2004
Second Printing, Revised Edition, 2007
Third Printing, Revised Tools of the Tree Edition, 2008

Lighten Up!

TABLE OF CONTENTS

A Note About
The "Energy Signatures"

The drawings in this book were created by Gayln Sweet, an artist who currently resides in Hawaii. She created them to express the spirit of each chapter of Part I. Thank you, Gayln, for your de *lightful* contribution and for gathering light together where we briefly landed: Sacred Grounds.

To those who have fallen
for the light.

"For I have eaten ashes like bread,
and mingled my drink with weeping."
-52nd Psalm

Introduction
Journey To Life!

I LIKE THE NUMBER 18. In Hebrew it's pronounced "chai," which also means *life*. Adult life begins at 18, and this book is about spiritual adulthood through liberation from frightening fantasy. The celebratory Jewish toast that says *"To life!"* summarizes this book's meaning, which is simply this: life is *for* you. Any thought that tells you otherwise denies true life.

I wrote this book to show you a way through your inevitable encounters with dark sorrow and crushing disappointment into the joyful light of a victorious life. *Part I* consists of 18 keys of light: may this number provide you with added support as you journey into your new and brighter *life*.

Part II presents a somewhat *lighter* approach, including light affirmations, aphorisms, exercises, and rhymes aimed at reinforcing and advancing the delightful changes in your life set forth in your journey through the first part.

Living Beyond Limits

This book reveals how to lose and what to lose for the ultimate gain. Every loss delivers a taste of that momentous occasion called "death" when you lose your whole world. That is why the deepest grief feels like dying and to fully re-enter life beyond grief's shore feels like being born anew.

To enter the life you really want may require nothing less than your movement through what feels like catastrophic loss. Deep sorrow signals your time for letting go has arrived. By loosening your grip on your life you lose its limitations. To leave your disappointment behind you simply have to release yourself from the situation that fosters it, and this book shows you how. But before you are willing to do that, you may have to suffer more, until you feel so fed up with holding on you are finally willing to let go.

As you let go of the imaginary, you enter the real, and leave all of your problems behind. You receive all of the joyful freedom and abundance your heart desires through the expansion of the four basic elements composing a great *L.I.F.E.*

LOVE

INTELLIGENCE

FAITH

ENERGY

Base your choices on what nurtures and expands these four essential elements within you. Then see that life does not just offer all you want; it *is* all you want, and it is endless. Thus, you emerge from a life that feels like death into a timeless life of limitless possibility, and I mean *limitless*.

No One Can Hold You Back

No one can hold you back from the life that you want. *No one but you.* You hold yourself back by holding onto an *imaginary* life that you don't want. All of the happiness, power, and abundance you desire flows into your life as you release your resistance to life right now. This expresses faith, and delivers the gift of faith.

The more faith you have in life, in what is happening right now, the greater your life. Period. Faith is the absence of a negative thought.

Faith releases you from fear-based thinking like, "I do not have enough time" or "I do not have enough money" or "I need more help than others are willing to give."

Faith emerges with the honesty to honestly face the unknown. The unknown cannot be feared, only the imaginary induces fear. The unknown is all you know.

When you count on anything but whatever is happening right now, you end up disappointed. You end up disappointed when you wait for what appear to be external circumstances to change before allowing yourself to live the free and joyful life abundant that is all that you desire, and which is always available, right now.

Release Yourself

If you know the signs to look for, you can tell if you hold yourself back from the life that you want. The first sign to look for is unhappiness. Unhappiness comes in many forms. You might be experiencing it right now in the form of loneliness, isolation, lack, unworthiness, injustice, dependency, discouragement, impatience, frustration, insecurity, or defeat. All of these signal that the time to *release yourself* has arrived.

The key to happiness is to let it happen, not to try to make it happen. We think that we lose our opportunity for happiness when we do not get our way, but as you will learn as you proceed through these pages, you actually *reject* happiness when you seem to lose it, and that rejects the very circumstances upon which you think your happiness depends. Happiness attracts every condition you want. When you feel happy you feel truly alive. Your body glows with wellbeing. Your mind sparkles with clear light. Your heart overflows with love. You expect things to work out and they do work out.

Happiness Tells You When You Are Getting It Right

Happiness is not about *getting* your way; it is about *finding* it. In happiness you are truly on your way. Unhappiness means that you have lost your way. Happiness flows with you as you flow with life. You oppose life when you lead a false life that you don't want. To leave the false for the true just see what you are really up to.

The person who envisions dismal futures, who imagines untrustworthy people, looks at life through the dark vision of a mind cut off from the heart. Happiness is the offspring of the heart and mind united. Any thought that takes you out of love kills your joy. Happiness retreats from the mind divorced from the heart.

Depression is born of thoughts that rob you of your faith. Under the spell of a heart and mind divided you believe you have to lead a false life, treat yourself and others cruelly, that unhappiness is necessary, responsible and right. Lose your heartless mind to find your happy, love-filled way. Unhappiness signals that you have fallen under the spell of a logical but abusive idea.

Do You Beat Yourself Down?

Beating yourself up doesn't lift you up; it beats you down. Holding onto the belief that you deserve unhappiness now is all that keeps joy from you.

Find your joy by first accepting the fact that you desire joy now. Then, look *within* to see how you keep joy from you. This accomplishes a crucial shift in perspective. Previously you looked outside of yourself for the cause of your unhappiness. But what appears as outside is just a reflection of what occurs inside!

The Secret of Happiness

Try looking at life through the eyes of faith for the vision of love to discover how truly wonderful your life is. The vision of love reveals that only good can come your way. When you expect something bad to happen, when you expect to be mistreated, when you expect to lose and fail and suffer defeat, *when you dread,* you peer into the visions of a heartless mind and reject the security, joy, love, and peace of the mindful heart. The heartless mind produces all of your misery, all the misery that exists.

Human beings have sought the secret of happiness for all time. The secret has remained concealed in the best hiding place of all: in the obvious. Well, here it is. Here comes that secret exposed. You need look no farther:

Don't Look For Facts That Support Faith; Look For Faith That Supports Facts!

The only proof you need that everything is bound to work out fine is found in your experience right now. You prove faith when you drop the fearful ideas that portray your life as a foe.

Seeing the mind's dark, frightening imaginings for what they truly are gives you a real high. This high differs from the high of certain drugs, like alcohol. These cause you to fall prey to a low that makes faith impossible and places your misery-producing illusions solidly in control.

Finding your way into real faith is not achieved through self-hypnosis, but rather, through de-hypnotizing yourself. Seeing your mental projections as the illusions they are releases your power to joyfully succeed at the highest levels.

You Have Arrived

You have arrived at the threshold of a world of limitless light. The time of ripeness is at hand, your ripeness for birth into a joyful life of boundless freedom. You are about to see life's previous pressures as a sort of womb that has been squeezing you out, pushing you into the real dimension of miraculous splendor, a world so wonderful that you will believe you found the key to heaven on earth. The longer you hold onto your imaginary burdens the more weightily they press upon you. When you let them go, you rise into the happiness that you futilely, desperately, and despondently sought by holding onto them.

Your frightening thoughts make life look unfaithful to you and then you lose your faith in life. Everyone would love to believe in love and you have probably tried believing in love yourself. If this belief failed you it is because you did not yet learn that lasting love finds you only in the light beyond the mind.

Paying closer, deeper attention to your feeling of life's heaviness returns you to life's lightness, the lightness of child's free heart. Then, you don't have to understand how life can equal love - *you experience it.*

Reversal

Boundless fulfillment eludes those who hunt for the symbols of accomplishment to prove their worth. You are already worthy of all you desire. You simply need to stop thinking of yourself as a person who needs to prove herself. People struggle and strive, hurry and worry, in a desperate attempt to make their lives work. They must fail at this because life already works. Their strenuous effort to control what does not need their control makes them miserable.

Happiness arrives through some basic reversals in our approach to it. One reversal involves looking at your reactions to life as a cause of what happens instead of as a result, something we explore in depth throughout this book. Another reversal involves relating to your so-called "troubles" as opportunities, opportunities for learning how you produce your trouble and how to stop.

The core reversal for happiness comes down to accepting joy *first*, not second. Allow yourself the happiness you desire *now* rather than waiting for some form of success to *make* you happy. Then you see how your happiness makes all of the success you want yours. As you read this book, you will not only learn how to do this; you will do it.

"The great thing is to persist to the end..."
-Fyodor Dostoevsky

Part I

18 Keys of Light

Key One

Faith and joy blossom
in the light beyond the mind.

LIGHTENING UP TAKES YOU to a world beyond the
thinking mind where joy, where miracles abound. There you
discover that you don't need anyone or anything to make you
happy, fulfilled, at peace, secure. You only need to enter the
light beyond your thinking mind. While you live in your
ideas about life, other people, and yourself, you cannot know
real happiness.

Why You Feel Down

Every time that you have counted on others or on circumstances to make you happy you eventually felt let down.
This happened because your false or thinking mind led you to
expect what cannot be. We make our fundamental mistake

regarding the quest for a happy life by pursuing happiness with the idea that we lack happiness. Your mind portrays you in a situation you don't want to be in; then you enter that illusion by relating to it as reality. As long as you live in illusion, you cannot know real happiness.

Letting Go

Happiness takes no effort. Our habit of making effort gets in the way. Finding happiness involves a letting go of effort – specifically, the effort to make oneself happy. It involves an acceptance of, an openness to, a trusting in what *is*. This requires our suspension of, or release from, the negative ideas we habitually project upon reality.

Happiness flows from the faith that surrenders fearful resistance to life's flow. Faith attracts, reveals, and opens doors of opportunity. Trust there is a way. *Know* there is a way. Soon, that way appears! In the meantime, learn how to live without worry. Faith is the absence of a negative thought

Living Faith

It takes faith to let yourself live naturally, to express the genuine you. Living in your natural rhythm, the action-rest pulse beat and daily pace at which you feel and function best takes faith.

You force yourself to rush in anxious pain and strain because your thinking mind tells you that you have to hurry and worry. Yet, life gets darker and heavier when you depart from the rhythm of your light way.

Living in the strain of pushing against life's flow produces your unhappy outlook through which life and people appear to be unfaithful, heartless, and cruel. You then tensely, anxiously, angrily brace yourself against the hard life that you imagine, which paves your way into that very hard life.

How you see life is a way that you treat yourself. Faith in life's essential goodness frees you to live in love and joy. Trust that you can treat yourself well and get away with it.

Reunite Your Mind And Heart

The infant demonstrates perfect faith. For the adult to experience that kind of faith, faith at the core, the mind of illusion must give way to a higher level of consciousness. Let's call that level, "*the mind of light*".

The infant's mind is only of light because ideas are not yet concretely formed, ideas that divide mind and heart. The infant does not worry about life until the child's thinking mind has been sufficiently formed and fashioned by fear. That probably happened to you. To reunite your heart and mind, remain alert to notice when your mental view of life, of a person, or of any particular situation takes you out of faith, love and joy.

Your loving thoughts invite into your heart the light of love that pours into you from beyond your thinking mind. But when your thought takes a downturn it blocks the light of love. Then you live in a dream of limitation in a loveless situation. When you see that *is* just a dream, you return to the infinite, where you live without difficulty, seeing difficulty as nothing but a habitual, straining reaction to the imaginary.

Life = Love

Ask yourself, "If life absolutely loves me, what would that tell me about what is happening to me right now?" The answer is simple. If life absolutely loves you, whatever is happening, even your heaviest sense of burden, deepest pain, and darkest dread, is in your best interest. Then F.D.R. misspoke – you have nothing to fear, not even fear.

To enter the light above the thinking mind is to know this absolute goodness that finally sets you free. To arrive there, practice viewing life through the eyes of faith. Your faith tells you that only good is possible. Your fear tells you that nothing good can come. Your faith tells you not only that you can receive miracles, but that you receive nothing less, not ever. Your fear tells you that good fortune is but a masquerade of impending disappointment.

Choose The Eyes Of Faith

Choose the eyes of faith by looking at your present circumstances and asking yourself, "How would faith see this?" Your faith tells you that every problem is really a solution. It tells you that even when life looks and feels all wrong it can still be all right. It tells you that even when you take the "wrong" road you end up on the right trip, in the right place.

The practice of looking at life through the eyes of faith equals looking through the vision of love. It lightens you up. It opens you to the light above the thinking mind. Upon your entry into that light you experience all of the joy, freedom, peace, and fulfillment you have been seeking everywhere but there – everywhere but here, *now*.

The Thinking Mind

You have, then, two levels of mind: one real and one false, a higher mind and a lower mind. We can call your thinking mind your false mind. This is the mind that symbolizes, represents, imagines. It produces sheer illusion. Its purpose is to serve the higher mind, to reflect its light of wisdom. But until we awaken to its illusory nature, we live trapped in the lies of the false mind and believe in its nightmare stories.

As you read this book, you are outgrowing the hold of the lower mind upon you; you are learning how to master that mind, a process that represents the next step, and maybe the last hope, for the human race. For as long as we live in the illusions of false mind, we live in fear of life, which drives us to destroy ourselves.

Your thinking mind can point you toward happiness, as it does through your reading of this book. But to experience happiness you have to awaken in the higher light, you must take a leap beyond the thinking mind, to look *at* it, not *from* it.

Your thinking mind generates appearances and automatic reactions to those appearances. It works like a TV. You see images on the screen of a juicy burger, and your mouth waters. You cannot eat *that* burger, but you want it just the same. All of your fears, desires, and attachments work like that.

In the light above your thinking, higher mind emanates wisdom, the intelligence of true love, the deeper knowledge of what is good for you. It descends into your awareness and guides you perfectly when you consciously observe your present experience.

Seeing The Thinking Mind At Work

Seeing the thinking mind at work takes you into the real light above it. It reveals the field of dream light in which your thinking mind casts its holographic images. Until this awakening, your thinking mind sinks you into the dark and troubled depths of anger, defeat, and broken hope.

Achieving your awakening beyond the thinking mind delivers you to the freedom and power to direct your thinking mind with loving intelligence. The creative power of your thinking mind then manifests conditions that match your heart's desire.

Find Your Way

You have to lose your mind – your thinking mind – to find your way – your true way. When you leave the blind tyranny of the lower mind you begin to live life your way, which is the one and only way of happiness for you.

You can follow your true way into joyful success in all areas of life. When you leave your true way you demand that circumstances and other people save you from your self-induced misery, which of course never works.

You lose your happy way when you try to fake it in any way, when you try to impress *anyone*. You lose your way when you make your happiness dependent upon *anyone's* approval, understanding, acceptance, or cooperation. You lose your happy way when you feel desperate for life to surrender to your will. You find your happy way by surrendering your resistance to life.

You lose your way by demanding that your dreams come true. You find your way when you trust that something greater than any dream you can imagine is all that can ever come true: *reality.*

Natural Laws Govern The Thinking Mind

Observing your thinking mind reveals the natural laws that govern all phenomena. For instance, you can see the law of inertia at work. You encounter mental inertia when you try to come up with a new idea, insight, or solution. You must apply some effort to set the mind's motion in the direction you want it to go. Apply the mental effort through an intentional focus of attention and eventually your idea comes, your insight unfolds, your solution dawns.

Another natural law of the mind can be described as the law of sowing and reaping. If you want to know something, decide to know it. This sows the seed of your intentional direction. In time, your intention bears fruit and the knowledge you have been seeking blooms in your conscious awareness.

Another natural law of the mind is the law of alternation. In nature, all conditions alternate from one opposite to the other. What goes up comes down. Breathing out follows breathing in. Night follows day. Any condition that arrives also passes away. Based on this law, if your thought of someone makes you like her today, a thought makes you dislike that person tomorrow. If you now believe, next you don't believe. If you feel sure about a decision you made today, tomorrow you have your doubts. You may argue for one point but then, when you least expect it, you can see the point you argued against. If now you see a reason to feel encouraged, soon you see a reason to feel discouraged.

As long as you live in your thinking mind you doom yourself to painfully bounce from pillar to post in the rough seas of alternating illusion. Every bright idea turns into dark uncertainty. No matter how hard you try to hold onto your positive thoughts, equally strong negative thoughts barge their way in. If your mind gives you a sense of victory now, you will soon fall back into your old, habitual sense of defeat.

The torture of living in the lower mind deepens over time. It makes you increasingly bitter, resentful, disappointed and discouraged until you cannot bear living in its limited world any longer. Then you have completed a major stage of the development of your lower mind, and you are ready, indeed, you are ripe, to...

Rise Above The Thinking Mind
And Awaken In The Light.

Just as you wake from sleep's dreams, you wake from unconscious living in thinking mind's illusions. This occurs naturally as you see *that* you think *when* you think. This clarifies the illusory nature of your thinking mind and of all your so-called "problems."

Awakening into *the mind of light* transforms earthly life into a dimension of heavenly life. It kills death and ends time. It dispels your nightmare visions of a loveless fate and unveils your greatest dreams – dreams almost to wonderful to believe in – and gives you faith in their coming true.

Until you wake up to what you are up to *within*, you cower before your depressing, fearful illusions. As you wake up, as you *lighten up*, you discover the power to choose your dreams and to have your most wonderful dreams come true.

Your Thinking Mind Leads You Astray

Your thinking mind leads you astray because it is not designed to lead, but rather to follow—to follow the direction given to it by your true or higher mind, the mind of faith, love, and wisdom. Consciously observe your thinking mind to receive guidance from your true or higher mind.

For your liberation into unlimited life, exchange your blind subjugation to your lower, thinking mind for direct conscious observation of that mind's activities. This requires getting accustomed to living without any clear idea of what is happening, because no idea of life *is* really happening.

Until you awaken from the dream-life of the thinking mind, you believe that life heaps upon you all the troubles that you only imagine. Living in that mind takes you to the point of utter desolation, when you feel dead inside after losing yet again. When you finally reach that point, if you just hold on and simply pay close attention, you discover the great dawn behind the dark; you see that the arrival of what appeared to be your ultimate defeat brought your ultimate victory. The end of fear's dark tyranny has arrived and your true, great life by faith has begun.

"All unhappiness originates
in the urge to escape reality."
-Newton Dillaway

Key Two

Accepting, not possessing, allows happiness to be.

FREEDOM IS THE DIFFERENCE between accepting and possessing. The law of constant motion insists that all goes against your effort to hold on. Ownership exists in the mind only, a mental map without a territory. Since possession is sheer illusion, you can never really satisfy the drive to *have* anything or anyone. Striving to possess feeds only endless craving and its eternal emptiness.

Whatever and whomever you think you own really owns you because what happens to him, her, or it controls your thoughts and emotional reactions. Relating to anyone, anything, or any condition as *yours* compares to purchasing a mirage of an oasis in a barren desert.

You strive to possess based on the false belief that you need to control what lies beyond your control. When you accept the coming and the going, instead of futilely resisting it, you entrust your life to greater wisdom, joy, freedom, and love.

"Relationships Of Ownership"

"Relationships of ownership" is a phrase in a Bob Dylan song, referring to those Dylan describes as "condemned to act accordingly." Do you strive to act accordingly – according to the expectations of others – in a quest for their acceptance? Do you writhe in pain over memories of past words or deeds of yours, worrying they cost you another's admiration? Do you think you need to have, be, or do more to make yourself acceptable?

When you don't like yourself you direct the energy of self-denigrating rejection into yourself. When you don't like another person, *you do the very same thing:* you hold onto a mental image that causes you to react with feelings of rejection. And this happens when you do not like a particular condition or life-situation - you send an electric current of negative feelings characterized by denigration and rejection into yourself.

Rejection occurs in relationships of ownership because no person, object, or condition acts just the way you want all of the time, and you instinctively reject what you don't want. Acceptance of the way things are permits the healing of the painful wounds of rejection.

The Meaning Of Wealth

We commonly associate the concept of freedom with wealth. To be really wealthy is to be free from the need to possess any more. You give yourself that luxurious state of freedom, though, only through acceptance.

The Heart Of Acceptance

The only way to be the one you want to be is to learn how to accept yourself just as you are. For others to be just the way you want them to be, learn how to accept them exactly as they are. For your life to be just the way you want it to be, learn how to accept it just the way that it is.

True acceptance, as I mean it here, has nothing to do with settling for less. You accept yourself by letting yourself fully and freely inside your awareness. In other words, by becoming consciously aware of how you think, feel, speak, and act in the present moment you demonstrate real self-acceptance –acceptance of the experience of yourself.

This is the true heart of self-acceptance. It brings you into the light. Until you admit your present experience of yourself into your awareness, you reject yourself, causing you the pain of unworthiness and leading others to reject you too. But when you accept yourself, you find happiness and discover people trusting and accepting you.

True Acceptance Equals Awareness

When you worry about how someone else sees you, you stop accepting and start rejecting. But if you simply begin observing your present experience of yourself, paying particular attention to your present thoughts and feelings, you return to self-acceptance and delight in its inherent joyful freedom.

To find the joy of acceptance of another as he or she is, and the joy of acceptance of every event or condition as it is, start accepting your *inner* experience of each person or situation into your awareness. To reside in your conscious attention is to experience greater freedom.

You Can't Buy Happiness

Here is one truth you can rely upon: the universe changes everything. Whatever your present situation, it's already history. And yet, at the same time, nothing ever really changes. The truth remains that every experience passes away.

Every thought passes into oblivion. Every feeling of pleasure passes, as does every feeling of pain. Experience, when closely observed, travels in waves.

Commercial advertising would have you believe that you can buy real happiness. And you see images of happy people with what you want. But what is the truth? The truth is that we all suffer just as much soon after our purchases as we did before, and there is absolutely nothing anyone can do to change that. But we can learn to trust and accept the way things are, including our distrust of the way things are, and so find growing freedom and joy.

Happiness Enters With Acceptance

Accept your thoughts and your emotional reactions, your likes and dislikes, your loving and your hating, your hoping and your fearing, your confusion and your clarity, your regretting and your pining, your envying and your resenting, instead of futilely trying to hold onto a self that you are not. Accept your present moment of experience into your awareness to realize that holding on is all that holds you back.

Imagine the freedom of accepting everything and everyone just as all *is*... with perfect *trust* in the way all is. How joyous! That freedom finds you as you simply look within and examine the arising, presence, and passing of your thoughts and feelings. This simple act frees you from the self-punishing illusion of yourself deprived in any way.

Rejection

If you want to stop experiencing the pain of rejection, you cannot. Whatever you struggle against remains in your struggle. If you resent yourself for resenting, you simply refuse to let your resentment go. Impermanence comes to your rescue! Think of change as grace. It releases you from whatever is bothering you.

To let a condition *be* is to let it go. We fear letting things be as if that permits them to remain; but nothing stops the cosmic sea. When an unwanted condition returns, just observe your thoughts and feelings about it. You will soon see that what you do not want exists nowhere but in your mind. If you don't hold onto the thought of it, by worrying, you will watch it pass almost as soon as it arrives.

Allow every condition to be in your awareness. You need not resist the negative. Any condition you resist you actually refuse to relinquish. No problem lasts any longer than your thought of it, and thought disintegrates in a flash. You must repeatedly experience what you do not want until you have paid enough attention to make your whole life new.

To Have The Life You Want

To have the life you want courageously view your inner life of thought and feeling until you see your mental life for what it is: a parade of ideas, a dance of dream-shadows, an imaginary impostor of the real. Observing your mind allows it to naturally come to an alert state of rest, where you find peace, clarity, and joyful relief. Like a still pond reflecting a clear sky, your calm mind reflects the intuitive flashes of wisdom streaming from the light of higher mind. Each flash of light increases your joy, feeds your love. To know you as you truly are is to love you; just as viewing others behind the mask of your disturbing ideas projected on them is to love them; and to know your life, as distinguished from the imaginary life that you complain and worry about, is to love your life.

Do You Hide Your Greatness?

We sometimes play down our glorious true nature. We portray ourselves as weak, inferior, helpless, hopeless, stupid, dependent to make another feel better. We exercise such sneaky manipulation through false pretenses to manage another's insecurity.

You cannot be happy suppressing your greatness. You resent the person whose acceptance you pursue through self-degradation. You resent yourself for stooping to self-demeaning measures.

Trying to impress anyone is not the answer, either. You do not have to make your greatness known. You cannot. It glows purely through authentic self-expression. When you observe yourself desiring to prove you are anything to anyone, just observe that happening and smile as it passes, as every desire must. Holding onto a desire keeps us stuck in that desire.

Do You Put Others Down?

In unconsciousness we vainly seek to reclaim lost worth by denigrating others. Only in self-acceptance can you let this go. No one has the power to diminish another's infinite worth, however blind to it we might be. You ensnare yourself in your feeling of worthlessness by trying to pass it on to anyone. No one is *really* available to anyone except as someone to cherish.

Lost Thinking

A common attack of self-rejection occurs when we tell ourselves that we are lost, in a bind we cannot escape, in need of a formula we cannot figure out. Then we feel inadequate.

Telling yourself that you are lost deafens you to the inner voice of profound wisdom directing you right now. Holding onto the idea that you do not know what you are doing and where you are headed blinds you to the open way where you want to go.

Unconscious Parenting

Our problem with rejection begins with unconscious parenting. A parent unconsciously rejects a child when she relates to that child with a lack of present awareness of the child. To accept your child into your deep awareness reveals the sacred innocence of the child and permits that innocence to guide you in your relationship with that child.

The child whose parent relates to him unconsciously learns to reject himself, to lead a false life, to gravitate toward others who reject him.

It's Time To Raise Yourself

It's time to raise yourself from the point your parents left off. Until you pay enough attention to what is going on within you, you confuse the real you with your angry, fearful thoughts about yourself; the real other with your angry, fearful thoughts of that other; your real life with your angry, fearful thoughts about your life.

Live Life Your Way Now

Unfortunately, we presume that we have to wait until we have enough money, or enough cooperation, or enough recognition from others to live exactly as we choose. But your freedom to live your way now occurs spontaneously - your life proves to be exactly as you want it - when you admit your experience of life as it is right now into your awareness.

Are You Too Demanding?

You can tell how far someone has strayed from living life his way by the intensity and constancy of his demands, complaints, and pathetic pleas for assistance. That person holds onto his problems and refuses to let them go. Paying too little attention to his thoughts and feelings, he imagines that someone else has the power to set him free and is unconscious that he *imagines* this.

Think For Yourself

Examining your thinking leads you to think *for* yourself instead of thinking *against* yourself. To think for yourself means courageously questioning your own assumptions, observing your thoughts to see what your assumptions are. Ultimately, this lets you receive the light of wisdom's intuitive insight. To enter a better life, pay attention to your life as it is until you see how you create your own experience.

How To Live In Approval

Approval-seeking locks you into disapproval. It places you at the mercy of those who would manipulate you with disapproval. Trying to manipulate another with your disapproval keeps you in the dark state of disapproval as well. Instead of viewing your disapproval as a necessary opinion of someone for not getting something right, see it as your painful way of showing yourself that you are better off without it.

The joyful state of approval occurs naturally as you allow your thoughts and feelings to arise and pass on their own before your conscious, watchful attention. This tames your mind and brings it under wisdom's control. It reveals how we place happiness beyond our reach by seeking happiness in a way that makes us miserable. Anyone who disapproves of living in love, peace and joy right now condemns himself to sorrow.

You don't need anyone or anything to rescue you from disapproval and rejection. Look within instead of fearfully striving to fit in.

"What is this undistinguishable mist of thoughts,
which rise, shadow after shadow,
Darkening each other?"
-Percy Bysshe Shelley

Key Three

See your reaction as a cause
rather than as an effect.

WHEN AN EVENT TRIGGERS your reaction, your reaction triggers a subsequent event. The more energy flowing into your frustrated, anxious, unhappy reactions, the more troublesome, chaotic, and inharmonious the circumstances that follow. That explains why the less control you have over your reactions, the less control you seem to have over your life. As you pay closer attention to your automatic reactions, you see their purely illusory basis, which discharges their power over you. At the same time, by simply observing your thoughts and feelings as they arise and pass, your reactions settle down, enabling you to be more selective in your responses. Thus, your responses lead you into consequences that come closer to your goals. This gives you the sense of being in control.

God Counts Every Tear Before It Even Falls

When you examine your inner world of thought and feeling responses long enough, it becomes increasingly clear that nothing occurs by accident. The universe is guided by love, designed to provide you with just the conditions you need to work free of the reaction patterns that bar your way to the great, miraculous life your heart desires.

Life works with the mathematical precision of perfect forethought. Your current life-challenges trigger the automatic reaction patterns that draw more of the same your way. The degree to which you gain your freedom from those reactions, your life rises to a higher level.

The logical mind tells you that your reaction to an event follows the event, making you a victim of what happens to you; but let this idea go. Life knows what you need. When you observe your reaction knocking you out of your peace and poise, you see the actual cause of the situation to which you react. To raise the level of your circumstances, rise above your circumstances.

Your Hungry Reactions

While life wants to free you, your automatic reaction patterns want to keep you bound for more of the troublesome conditions on which they can feed. For example, the more you worry about your finances, the more you're drawn you into further financial difficulty, giving you the temptation to worry even more.

Your inharmonious emotional reactions don't want you to find release, because then they would cease. They seem to have an instinctive survival drive of their own. They operate like ravenous, wild animals bent on growing stronger by consuming more of your life force. The stronger and longer your reaction, the more life force you feed it.

You Are Not The Angry You

Paying closer attention to your reactions soon reveals their mirage basis, so that you take them less seriously and they take less energy from you. One interesting thing you see is this: immediately before you react in, say, an angry way, an image flashes on the screen of your mind, a mental image of you reacting with anger. If you identify with that angry image, it takes you over and you want to react in destructive ways aimed at feeding your angry reaction and making it stronger.

At the same time, it becomes obvious that you can just as easily choose to let that mental image pass as a possibility you do not select, and, instead, remain in the joy of peace and love, guided by wisdom, to serve your real interests, rather than giving yourself over to the angry image and serving *it* as its slave.

Taming The Beast

Each time that you look at your internal reaction instead of unconsciously identifying with it, you see the truth of its false nature and allow it to pass more quickly, depleting its food supply. Gradually, the intense emotional reaction that once devoured your energy, emotions, body, thoughts, and *life* like a hungry lion, now gently prances through the light of your consciousness like a playful kitten, slightly pesky perhaps, but posing no real danger. No longer driving you into destructive action, it leaves you in peace, freer to choose responses in line with your true goals.

Freeing The God In You

Have no fear that loosening the grip of your destructive reactions upon you leaves you weaker, more passive, or any less passionate. Those who react most stressfully, angrily, anxiously, and unhappily suffer the gravest health problems. Your

power will flow into your health and vitality, energizing your
love, gratitude, insight, and inspiration, increasing your moti-
vation to work and your will to work more efficiently, effec-
tively, and joyfully. You will be freeing the God in you.

As you release yourself from your old angry, fearful, discouraging reactions you achieve liberation from their dark
power to lure you into circumstances that prompt you to give
them more of your energy. In other words, they lose their
power to send you where you do not want to go.

A Formula For Success

To exchange your failures for success, surrender resistance
to your circumstances. Just observe your experience in the
present. Things only go wrong in your mind. The situation
you resist is one that does not actually exist. Look within for
the imaginary condition that triggers your resistance. When
you find it, watch it dissipate. This constitutes a secret inner
formula for success.

The Mental "Hall Of Blame"

Those who do not examine enough the motion pictures
streaming through their minds closely enough operate from
illusion. They fight imaginary villains and suffer the losses of
imaginary victims. Their reactions to their unconscious fantasies give their oppressive circumstances more power over
them.

Let's say that you feel frustrated because of time con-
straints. Look more closely at why you feel how you feel and
you discover that you feel frustrated as long as you imagine
yourself in that tight spot. Treating that illusion as real generates your frustration and creates the illusion of even more
restrictive confinement. As you release yourself from your

internal pressure you find yourself easily doing exactly what you need to do by the time it needs to be done.

Let's say that you feel angry over the unfairness of you being the only one of your friends who is not in a loving, harmonious, intimate relationship with a "significant other". By looking more closely at what you are really reacting to, you discover it to be nothing but a mental image of a life you do not want. You see further that the more you relate to that image as your reality, the more unhappy and lonely you become. But the more you see that image for what it really is, the more quickly and easily you let it go and the freer you find yourself to choose the life you want.

The next time that you feel annoyed over another person's actions, pay closer attention to your reaction to see that blaming your annoyance on that person deepens your experience of powerless dependency and generates more annoyance. Hanging any imaginary pictures in your "mental hall of blame"?

The Illusion Of Conflict

You engage more trouble by reacting *against* what happens. Your present experience turns out to be all that you really want it to be when you pay it enough attention. You see, for instance, that your loving response serves every need, solves every problem, and that life always presents you with the opportunity to live in a loving way. All you don't want is the negative way you react to the negative possibilities you imagine. To exit *any* bothersome condition, direct your energy into loving measures and you are out, because loving is all you really want.

Conflict exists in your mind only. You imagine someone or something against you and that pits you against. The beginning of every conflict's end occurs when you see your mind holding onto imaginary conflict.

Look at what happens when you complain that you do not receive the help you need. The emotional energy surrounding that idea draws you into situations in which you feel increasingly powerless, helpless and dependent.

We can sum up the way you bring trouble upon yourself as follows: affirming life's opposition to your interests fosters your experience of life's conflict with your desires.

Verbal Sticks And Stones

Remember the old saying, "Sticks and stones may break my bones but words can never harm me"? It's a lie. What you say to yourself and hear from others can prove deadly.

A dear friend of mine committed suicide a while back because, as she wrote in her farewell note, she saw no future for herself. I wonder if she talked herself out of recognizing that seeing no future was telling her to live fully in the present and give up some control. The future is a fantasy that only fools believe in, anyway. Sacrificing living fully in the now for a future that does not exist makes no one happy.

What Are You Talking Yourself Into?

Negative verbal affirmations feed and strengthen negative emotional reactions, increasing their power to draw you into circumstances that you don't want. Tell yourself that you are trapped in a horrible marriage and you feel increasingly trapped. Tell yourself that you have no reason to live and leaving life seems to make more sense. Declare that things won't work out and you plunge yourself deeper into despair. The moment after you refer to someone as your enemy, you feel more threatened. Emotionally complain about how another let you down and you feel more disappointed and disgusted. You talk yourself into what you say.

Positive Verbal Affirmation

A conscious, constructive application of verbal affirmation talks you into a brighter life. Speak more consciously. When you feel tempted to declare a condition that you do not want to be in, choose silent self-investigation instead. You will see that you are about to hypnotize yourself into treating an imaginary condition as real. This gives you a little more freedom to think about the condition you want, and to come up with a loving way to proceed for it.

Positive, carefully crafted affirmations can help you direct your creative energy into materializing the conditions that you want. When you affirm what you want to be true, you talk yourself into it.

For example, affirm, "I am on the right track" and you immediately start looking for the conditions in your life that support that statement. This directs you *to* the right track. Affirm, "Life now offers me all that I desire" and you begin looking for facts that make that statement true, which sends you into that reality. Affirm to your sweetheart, "You are my gift from heaven," and you begin seeing how true that is.

The key to using verbal affirmation constructively is to use the power of your words more and more consciously. Then you can construct your statements according to the actual results that you observe. Those who assert that affirmation does not work do not know what they are talking about. I don't need anyone to agree with my observations. When I softly repeat, "Peace, peace, peace" to myself I feel more at peace in the now.

The Practical Limits Of Affirmation

Confusion about the power of verbal affirmation begins when we make too much of it. Stating that there is a limit to

the power of verbal affirmation does not diminish the power
of affirmation. Nothing you can say about affirmation will
give you the power to talk yourself into growing another head
in the next five seconds. Nor do you need to react with terror
when you hear or say a negative affirmation.

A conscious, disciplined application of verbal affirmation
can help you make a *slight* shift, and every little shift helps.

Speak Responsibly

Affirmations are not always audible. Paying attention to
your mind gradually discloses the negative statements that you
silently make. "This guy is a jerk," you might be thinking.
Paying close attention to the impact of that remark reveals that
it deepens your pain of disdain. Negative mental affirmations
like, "There is not enough time" or "It's too late" or "I don't
have what it takes" or "I don't deserve what I want" talk us out
of faith.

What you say and how you say it influences what happens
to you next. Don't take my word for it. Pay closer attention
to your verbal experiences to witness the undeniable truth of
this. You will see, for instance, that we mistakenly presume
that we really have no choice but to verbally cut and complain,
that this is really something that we do to ourselves that is not
working, and that we have the freedom and power to do something else.

"The universe seems planned for good."
-Elbert Hubbard

Key Four

You belong where you find yourself.

THE KEY IS TO *find* yourself. This occurs as you let go of any idea of who you are and focus direct awareness onto your present state of being, onto your present experience of yourself. This automatically releases unnatural tension as awareness guides you into harmonious living.

As long as you identify with your mental concepts and pictures of yourself, you remain lost, separated from yourself and your true path by the veil of thinking mind's illusion. The moment you find yourself, you find your way. The more tense, nervous, discouraged, frustrated, or anxious you feel, the less you are in touch with yourself; you are in touch with the pain of leading a life that clashes with you.

If you let thought run your life, it ruins your life. Your ideas shape your experience. Paying attention to your thoughts alerts you to the shape of things to come. Your direct awareness of your present experience of yourself guides you in the right direction, including the right direction of thought.

Let Belonging Guide You

You belong where your needs are met, in a state of perfect harmony, and nowhere else. See how your choices take you out of there. Your direct awareness of your present experience of yourself leads you from a life of longing into a life of belonging. It automatically takes you to where you truly fit in.

Resisting pain deepens pain. Relief arrives as you observe your resistance. Then you find the peace that belongs to your release from unnaturalness. All tension is unnatural, a sign that you have slipped out of the shape you belong in.

The Illusion Of Elsewhere

You feel lack, oppression, and unhappiness when you think you belong elsewhere. Belonging exists only where you are. When you accept this, you enter the miraculous where you are. You experience the miracle *that* you are.

"Elsewhere" is an illusion. Longing for it robs you of what you want right here. It robs *you* from where you are. You long for another condition at the expense of the condition you belong in. You long yourself out of harmony.

The idea of there being a "better" situation for you demeans your present in its false shadow. You now have the opportunity to enter a new life of greater love, intelligence, faith, and energy. But you have to accept where you are to find it.

Clinging And Resistance

You cling and resist your way right out of belonging and into deeper longing when you imagine a better place to be.

Trusting where you are sets you free. As long as you imagine something missing, your fear makes it so, because you bring about what you think about. You struggle to control what does not need your control, being already under perfect control. You cling to the pain of clinging and resist the pleasure of releasing because you imagine that you must and fall for that fantasy.

You cling to whom and to what does not belong with you – at least as long as you cling. You resist what and whom you can never really avoid, evade, or escape – as long as you resist. Clinging and resisting go wrong for you, though you employ them to get what you think is right for you. To cling is to resist freedom, and to resist is to cling to restriction.

You Cling To The Wrong Reason

You cling to the wrong reason *for* the wrong reason. For instance, you cling to the reasons why your job is wrong for you, thinking and speaking of them over and over, based on the fear that if you let go of how wrong it is you will let yourself remain stuck there forever. Yet, clinging *keeps* you in the wrong condition. You can follow belonging to ever more rewarding work.

You cling to the reasons why your spouse is wrong for the false pleasure of feeling right, but that only makes you feel worse about your spouse. You distrust others to protect you from future betrayal, but that just keeps you locked in the betrayals of the past.

When you observe the pain of resisting your present freedom to live in harmony and peace, you discover that it's already a condition of the past. When you free a person or condition from your idea of being wrong, you can love right now.

We cling to what was and resist change, imagining that the past held more promise. But its promise is fulfilled in the present. You are moved at the precise instant that you no longer belong where you were. When you no longer belong where you are, nothing and no one can keep you here.

Your Perfect Opportunity

To find yourself where you truly belong, live consciously. Trust where you are. Accept it as your perfect opportunity to be free. This draws to you all things needful.

Pining over missed opportunity conceals the perfect opportunity always present. However things work out, now presents all you really need. You can go anywhere from here. Let the disappointing idea that you would have been better off *"if only"* pass. You gain nothing by relating to what *is* as any less than all you want it to be.

You belong in a life lived your way, doing what inspires you, open to the fulfillment of the now. Living in conflict with life never works. Being your own perfect opportunity, you need only to let yourself be.

How To Right All Wrongs

We wrong ourselves when we cling to the idea of being *wrong* and *wronged.* Notice when you feel *wrong* because of what you have done or failed to do, because of what you have or lack. Notice when you feel wronged by another. Notice when you try to make another feel wrong, or when you make another wrong in your mind. *Examine these experiences of wrong feeling to see how quickly you can let them go.*

What we are looking at here is the sense of betrayal, which exists only in realm of deception. You live in the illusion of betrayal as long as you overlook *your choice* to live in it.

Paying Attention To Your Inner Life

Paying attention to your inner life reveals the way out of all forms of betrayal. You can think of yourself prospering as easily as you can imagine getting ripped off. You can picture yourself succeeding as easily as you can picture yourself failing. You can picture yourself in a loving relationship as easily as you can imagine someone cheating on you. And you bring about what you think about. Thinking fearful thoughts is a sign that it is time to direct your thinking, or to let your thinking go.

The way out of feeling like a wrong person living a wrong life in a wrong world opens for you as you release yourself from thoughts of wrong. Living fully in this moment attunes your mind to wisdom, your heart to love and courage, and your actions to bold success.

Lose What You Fear

When you imagine that you would be better off in some other set of circumstances, you place yourself in the precise situation you want out of. Our problem is that we hold onto what we fear, as though we belong to fear, which we do not. The instant that you really look at what you fear, you see it is illusion. This sends you back into reality.

You cling to the frightening idea of landing in trouble by resisting the trouble you imagine, which ensnares you in that trouble. Releasing the frightening possibilities that you cling to leaves you with nothing left to fear. Losing longing sets you free from the depressing assumption that you really need what you don't have. Lose longing by letting it move through you until its wave of anguish is done. You lose the depressing notion of your life's pointlessness by seeing it for what it is: nothing but a joyless perspective you keep running through your mind to torment yourself, like running your tongue across the sharp, jagged edge of a broken tooth over and over again.

You live in the world you worry about until you notice your way out of the worry by examining your worries until you discern their destructive function and illusory nature. This automatically raises you above worry, at least for the moment, demonstrating the magic of awareness. And each moment's release takes you higher, until the worry that used to drown you is nothing but a shallow, babbling brook you can skip over. The deeper and darker the worry you get through, the higher you rise all together above the emotional gravity of dread.

You Receive More Of What You Focus On

You don't belong in longing. That's why it hurts so. Longing makes you feel dependent, lost, helpless, and hopeless. It manufactures the loss that you long to leave because it projects it upon your experience. The thick film of your misinterpretation deprives you of the direct life-experience of fulfillment. Yet, your present experience leaves nothing to be desired. Even longing turns into fulfillment if you accept it as your current experience.

The false idea and false feeling that tell you your present is worthless will leave if you let them. They remain only as long as you resist their flow. Focus on your present experience, whatever it is, to experience more life, understanding, inspiration, freedom, and power. Thus you enter the state of belonging from longing for all your needs to be met.

The Law Of Reversal

Life flows up and down in waves and it never stands still. Your current situation is bound by law to reverse itself. You don't have to turn your loss into your gain. Your loss will turn into gain by law and you grow into more in the process. By living in fearful resistance, though, you impede life's flow and get stuck in the muck.

Decide upon what you want. It will happen, because you truly do belong where you truly want to be. The loss you go through prepares you for the gain. If the process seems stalled, prepare for an accelerated launch. Drop the logic that argues for depression and foresees the impossibility of your miracle. *Stop mentally projecting limits upon the miracle of your creation.* Conditions beyond your control don't require your control. If you're going through a downturn, look for the upturn.

Whatever goes up goes down. Each fall turns into a rise. You don't have to make this happen. It happens by law.

Beyond Your Control?

Aren't you always beyond your control? Just observe yourself closely to realize this. You can't stop aging. You never seem to get enough done. You long to be in two or in twelve places at once.

Your actions demonstrate your limitations. You believe that you would no longer worry if you could just make something else happen, like if you made more money. But that something never happens. Or by the time it does, you have found something new to worry about. So you continue to work for what you think you need to live without worry, when all you need is to let worry go.

Worry is the prelude to greater peace, as pain is the prelude to greater pleasure.

How To End Up

Human beings are like rubber balls: the harder we hit bottom, the higher we rise. In fear's illusion we make ourselves into bottom-dwellers, though, by clinging to what we have left for fear of falling farther. This turns the floor into our ceiling.

You have to feel totally done with your life to be ready, willing, and able to let go of the life you have for the life you have been praying for. You cannot embrace the new holding onto the old. By law your life heads into fulfillment.

The Fire Of Desire

Desire, like longing, is a prelude to fulfillment. Live within the fire of desire as long as it blazes. Don't fear it or fight it or seek to extinguish it in any way. Let that fire fill you and watch it melt away the illusion of your separation from all that you desire.

Wake Up To Your Desire

Events instantaneously align with the fulfillment of your desire. The instant that you desire anything, you belong in that experience of desire. The more you resist what happens, the more you desire to resist.

You *always* get what you want. However, unconscious desires are always negative, because we desire more pain to wake us up. Unhappy people desire their unhappiness. Frustrated people desire their frustration. Anxious people desire their anxiety. Don't take my word for this. Just observe yourself more closely to see that you choose the state you're in.

When you wake up to what you desire, you *automatically* desire and receive a better life. Look within for what you *really* want. You'll find yourself fulfilled.

*"...we find ourselves in a condition which,
even if it seems to drag us down and oppress us,
yet gives us opportunity, nay, even makes
it our duty, to raise ourselves up..."*
-Wolfgang von Goethe

Key Five

Failure is an illusion.

YOUR IDEA, CONCEPT, or opinion of an event, a condition, an outcome, a person occurs on such a subtle level that you may not realize that it presents you with a counterfeit reality, a flickering form of illusion veiling the infinite cosmic instant. Then, based on your emotional reaction to the confines of your unconscious notion, you superimpose a value, function, meaning onto the limitless. This constitutes living in a dream.

How you interpret what happens turns it into your obstacle or opportunity. For instance, you can treat a disappointment as a reason to give up or treat it as an opportunity to build the strength of your persistence. Choosing the former option turns your past into your future. Choosing the latter places your future under your control.

"Failure" Is A Frame Of Mind.

When you regard yourself as a failure you fail yourself, as long as you identify yourself with that negative frame of mind. You experience failure by imagining it. Accepting that experience when it comes, examining it, and not giving up turns you into an unstoppable success. Every event equals opportunity.

The universe works by law and order, even when chaos appears to reign. Take action in line with your intended outcome and that outcome arrives at last. You receive what you want (even when you don't). You achieve what you work for. You cannot seek without success.

Let Hope Go

Holding onto hope does not protect you from hopeless despair. It prevents you from ever really getting anywhere. Look beneath hope and you will find insecurity lurking there, feeding on despair.

At the end of holding onto hope find peace, grounded in positive expectation, trust in the good basis of any outcome, belief in the miracle of life. Your state of mind equals the state of your life.

What You Call "Failure"

What you call "failure" actually delivers your success in the mental wrapping of a self-defeating idea. You imagine failure out of habit. Unwrap the present and receive your gift!

When you feel frustrated, anxious, or disappointed, look for the source within. Ask yourself, "What imaginary condition am I responding to?" Then examine your mind to discover the real cause of your drama. You must imagine something wrong to feel anything but right.

Success Is All That's Left

Success is all that's left when your mind clears of illusion -
success, inspiration, fulfillment, delight. Unconscious imagining conceals the success of life that is your very being so unlimited and free.

It takes alert awareness to notice the presence of a habitual
imaginary vision of failure's bleak charade. It requires the will
to be conscious of your mind's activities. Emotionally reacting
depletes the energy you need to stay conscious. Paying attention to your reactions takes back your power to be aware, bring-
ing the mind under your control. In awareness you automatically steer your life along the course of true success.

Rest Attentively

When you feel very emotional, relax, let go, and rest *atten-
tively*. My teacher, Isidore Friedman, called this a state of "focused
relaxation and attention without tension". If you slip off to sleep,
so be it. You will replenish your power of vigilant command over
your mind, which translates into command over your life.

We have grown roots in our pathetic sense of the failure of
life. As you awaken from the dream-state that produces failure, you enter the light where your greatest dreams come true.

Life Beyond Limits

Jane's lover passed away. She felt devastated. Upon looking within, she saw a mental movie of the end of her happiness and fulfillment in love. She saw that movie as the source
of her pain and said to herself, "How do I know that we will
not be together again, after a brief pause, to complete the journey of the heart we started?"

Hugh feared death. Then he looked more consciously at
his mind and he saw that he feared the imaginary. "To know

the true nature of death, I need to let go of mere conjecture," he mused. He continued paying attention, now, to his present experience, and peacefully thought, "All I really know right now is this endless moment of life. Why deny myself of this fulfilling experience in exchange for an imaginary loss?"

Angel felt depressed because she believed that she did not have time to achieve her goals. She looked at her mind and saw that her depression came from the logical seduction of imaginary boundaries. The exciting realization then occurred to her, "Time is an illusion that denies us of eternity." She wondered if she had made it to heaven already.

When You Feel Deprived

When you feel deprived, depressed, or disheartened you view a mental movie and get caught up in its plot, then suspend your belief in life. You picture your fate falling short of a miracle and fall for that horror story. You leave life to live in a pathetic, demoralizing vision of defeat. Distinguishing between a thought's movie and direct awareness of present experience turns your darkness into light.

When Things Don't Seem To Go The Way You Wanted

When things don't seem to go the way you wanted stop comparing your experience and start entering it. You'll discover all you want right here. For all you really know, everything is turning out better than you had hoped. See the phantasmagoria of thought for the string of illusions it is to leave the nightmare of loss, lack, and limitation. Nothing but what you seek sets limits on what you find.

Lose False Dependency

When someone lets you down, you did not really need his support in the form you thought you did. What you wanted from him would have fortified the walls of your prison of false dependency. By law, everyone is bound to give you precisely what you need from them.

Everyone arrives to set you free. The more you depend upon others the more they disappoint you. Stop telling yourself that your greatest opportunity is not present. Your greatest opportunity is to face your own fear. When God does not give you your way, God tells you it's time to develop your power to make your way, which is what you really want anyway. Cast off the idea of yourself as weak to discover that you're strong.

Bob Dylan wrote, "He not busy being born is busy dying." This reminds me to continue growing into someone new for something more. When someone lets you down, ask yourself, "What does this call upon me to make of myself?"

All You Really Want Is Happiness

Happiness equals true success. If you felt happy enough, you could love everyone. You would be undefeatable. Happiness is a sign of real power. You put off happiness as long as you think you need certain things to happen before you can be happy. Accepting happiness first brings all you want. Happiness glows within you as you recognize and release the habitual ways that you resist it.

The Success That You Desire

The success that you desire remains separated from you as long as you imagine it away. You enter happy success when you stop holding onto your belief in the division between you and your goals. You live happily ever after when you let go of your ways of living without happiness. Counting on conditions to bring you happiness puts off those very conditions. Happiness empowers you to create the conditions you want. Happiness makes you irresistible, healthy, strong, vibrant, beautiful, resourceful, optimistic, *successful.*

Desperation

Desperation on the other hand, draws you deeper into loss, lack, and sad limitation. The person or condition that you desperately pursue retreats by law. Find your own completion in happiness by consciously experiencing your present; then you became the pursued. Why do you suppose it happens this way? By law every condition seeks completion.

Lose desperation by allowing yourself to experience it consciously as long as it lasts, without holding onto it or pushing it away. Then, what you have been seeking finds you.

You Can Be Nothing But Successful

Your desire and intention define the path that your life takes. Thinking yourself into misery forms the instrument of your tragedy.

Your feelings of love, joy, contentment, and completion define your miracle. Let beliefs that negate its existence go. You succeed at all times. You feel like a failure as long as you want to. You see your life, your wife, your child, your job, your financial condition as a disappointment as long as you choose to. You can be nothing *but* successful.

You succeed at driving others away by trying to get something from them, because they must instinctively resist the lack of your gain. This keeps you in the best position to develop greater self-reliance.

Peace, Power, And Plenty

Think about how you would love your life to be. Then think about how happy you would feel if you knew without a doubt that your life is always infinitely better than you could ever hope for it to be. That gives you a peek into the miraculous, heavenly existence lying in wait for you, behind the imaginary dark existence your thinking mind habitually and unconsciously projects onto the screen of your awareness. Achieving liberation from that projection equals the pinnacle of success, and it is not as difficult to achieve as you might think. In fact, it is easier to achieve than a thought, because it requires no thought to achieve.

If you feel unhappy, deprived, hopeless you unconsciously live in disturbing visions of your undoing. No one can do the right thing as long as she believes life does her wrong. Peace, power, and plenty expand in your life as you see through the illusion that anything less than all you desire can be.

Think about all that you want, all that it would take to make you feel absolutely happy, secure, content, in love, and fulfilled right now. Then ask yourself, "What would be infinitely greater?" as you open your heart, your consciousness, your life to the answer. Then affirm, "The present is infinitely greater than any condition I can imagine."

Happiness Is The Key

Happiness is the key that unlocks life's treasure chest. And yet, we count on unhappiness to get us our rewards. We rely on hurry and worry. We push ourselves so hard that we harden our hearts and close our minds to any better options.

We unconsciously confuse our painful memories with our present possibilities, as Chekhov wrote: "And this constant dissatisfaction with herself and everyone else, this succession of bad mistakes that loom up like a mountain before you whenever you look back on your past, she would accept as her real life, her destiny, and she would expect nothing better."

Or we seek release through misery, as Chekhov writes elsewhere: "It's all so clear: in order to live in the present, we should first redeem our past, finish with it, and we can expiate it only by suffering, only by extraordinary, unceasing labor." As long as you feel the need to go on suffering, you will do so. If you do so consciously, examining your experience, you see that it lasts no longer than you really want it to.

What Do You Count On?

Unhappy people count on need to succeed. In this universe of law and order, if you plant a seed in decent soil, nurture it properly, and wait, it sprouts. But one of life's laws is not need. You cannot *need* anything badly enough to make it happen. The more you need, the more you need. But you can suffer enough to find joy, for in suffering lies the key to joy.

When you examine your suffering you discover the cause of your suffering. Unconscious suffering is the key to nowhere.

What do you count on to take you where you want to go? Do you count on sorrow and pain? Do you realize that can never work?

What alternative do you have? Your unhappiness dissipates as you embrace it, examine it. When you look for your miracle in whatever *is* you join the ranks of the truly wise, and wisdom, success, and happiness go together.

"...to the rightly perceiving mind, there is the same infinity, the same majesty, the same power, the same unity, and the same perfection, manifest in the casting of the clay as in ... the kindling of the day-star."
—John Ruskin

Key Six

When you feel down, ask yourself, "What am I up to within?"

YOUR INNER WORLD operates like the world appearing outside you. Thought and feeling events enter your field of attention just as physical sensory events such as the scent of fresh baked cookies, the sound of a lawnmower, the sight of a shadow cast by a cloud.

The events of your life seem random, until you start paying closer attention. Cause-effect relationships then gradually become clear. Angry people gravitate to other angry people, who inevitably produce destructive dramas. Peaceful people gravitate to other peaceful people who tend to create harmonious situations.

Inner Attunement
Your thought-feeling world works similarly. Angry feelings attract angry thoughts, which send you into more angry feelings. Peaceful, loving feelings attract inspiring, loving

thoughts, which bring you more peaceful, harmonious feelings.

Your basic state of feeling, which we can call your inner attunement or vibration, attracts the thoughts and feelings you receive. You can tell your basic vibrations by the quality of thought and feeling you live in.

The Inner Cause

Your thoughts and feelings drive you into life conditions that match their vibration. Consciously viewing the thought and feeling events that occur to you gradually gives you control over your "inner world", and that gives you control over what appears to happen in your outer world.

Superficial observation leads one to presume that chaotic life conditions cause chaotic mental and emotional reactions. Paying closer attention to your experiences reveals, however, that your chaotic mental and emotional states produce, sustain, and exacerbate chaotic life conditions.

When we feel unhappy, we typically look for an external cause. "I feel depressed because I don't have enough money," is an example of this. But this leads one astray. You enter disturbed inner states because you are attuned to them and unconsciously overlook your opportunity to let them go by.

Claim Your Inner Freedom

Imagine walking into a bar and observing a heated altercation between two enraged individuals. You can remain in the bar, even enter the fray, or leave. Unless you have some good reason to stay there or to get involved (like if you are a policeman), your best option would probably be to turn around and leave, wouldn't it?

You have the same freedom of choice when it comes to your thoughts and emotional states. You can view the condition and decide whether or not it is really a condition you wish to get engaged with. You do not have to get involved.

Awareness Gives You Freedom

The degree of your conscious awareness makes all the difference here. You see, some people are so unconscious, so numb to their experience, that they might enter the bar and sit right next to the fighting drunks without noticing the obvious danger. They might even order a drink or two, diminishing their power of sensitive discernment. Before they know it, a bottle comes crashing on their head. Then they really get mad because they think of themselves as "an innocent victim" unjustly treated (if they have any consciousness left to think with after that head-blow).

Similarly, we can be so unconscious and numb to our inner experience that we do not realize a negative thought and feeling has arrived before we automatically engage in it.

As You Practice Being More Aware

As you practice being more aware of your present experience, you discover more and more freedom of choice as to which person, place, or situation ("outer world" condition) you get involved with, and also, which thought and feeling ("inner world" condition) you engage, and which ones you let go of.

The more you let go of angry, discouraging, and frightening "inner conditions", the more harmonious the life-conditions you attract. At the same time, the more peaceful, loving, happy thoughts and feelings you attract, which lead you into more harmonious circumstances in life.

Losing Negativity

We can define negativity as an attitude of *against* what is. Negativity says, "This is against me; therefore I stand against it."

You turn a negative state into a positive one by simply observing it. Observing it takes your power out of it. Nature does the rest. Just as water naturally comes to rest when you stop stirring it up, your thoughts and feelings come to rest when you consciously let them be.

Negativity carries with it high costs. Living in a disturbed inner state makes it impossible to create more order in your life. Negativity generates trouble. Yet, we resort to it when trouble arrives as if it will repel the trouble it attracts.

When People Express Negativity

When people express negativity they do not always know it. They might even believe they are happy while they smoke, drink, and eat too much; as they exercise too little and work too hard; as they lash out at those they love because they blame their thoughts and feelings on some outside source.

We instinctively leave pain, but first we have to recognize that we are in pain. Then we need to discover the actual source. Feeling the pain of burning heat will not help you much if you do not realize that the pain is caused by your proximity to a flame. Thinking that someone else makes you angry, that your financial condition makes you feel discouraged, that your mate's behavior makes you feel insecure, will not help you either. You automatically relate to negative thoughts and feelings as external reality. There lies the source of your pain.

To See Your Negativity

To see your negativity begins your liberation. The next time that you express resentment, hostility, or critical condescension, focus your attention on your thoughts, feelings, speech, and actions. Observing yourself closely soon reveals that *you* are really the target and the victim of your wrath.

Seeing your negativity hurts because negativity holds pain. Seeing it requires the courage to face your pain, when instinctively you want to flee from it. But until you face it you won't see the actual cause of it, and seeing the cause of it sets you free.

If you feel stuck in a relationship with a negative person, look for the negativity in you. Letting go of your negativity lets negative people go.

A Loveless Lie

A negative attitude is an attitude that makes you unhappy. It depresses you with a loveless lie. You don't have to regard all conditions as equal in every way to find happiness; simply trust all experience as intrinsically equal and all together good. From that basis you can judge this or that as inferior in a relative sense, within a limited context, without driving yourself out of joy.

Is Anything Wrong?

You have to imagine something going wrong for you to experience something wrong. Even when you feel wrong or wronged, for all you know everything is all right.

"But it may *not* be all right," you might argue. The fact is that you don't know, though, do you? And releasing negative speculation leaves you feeling all right.

You worry that if you don't fight against a wrong the wrong continues, but that just lures you into a fight. Some people think that they like to fight. They'll fight you if you give them the chance. Some of them even think they fight for peace. They will do all they can to deny you of peace if you spend much time with them.

Your Miraculous Release

You think that your circumstances make you feel stuck, but only holding onto the notion of being stuck keeps you in that spot. The more you think of someone as your enemy, the more power over your life you give that person. Focus on raising yourself instead of downing a foe. No weaker force can overcome a greater. He who goes through your assaults consciously grows stronger and smarter.

The miraculous promise of your life fulfills you the instant you stop imagining yourself in any lesser condition.

How To Live Beyond Your Expectations

We used to believe that negativity is the necessary and right reaction when things don't go as we had hoped. Our parents behaved this way and that subconsciously taught us to regard it as natural.

One thing the parents of many of us did not teach is that events falling short of our expectations present us with the opportunity to see how we make ourselves miserable.

The better you handle what you don't want, the better it becomes, until you turn it into all you want. You think things need to work out a certain way, but even when they don't, they happen the way you need them to.

False Anger

Philip became angry when his girlfriend gave him incorrect driving directions. He thought of her as undependable. Then he accepted the challenge of finding his way on his own. He succeeded and felt more self-reliant in the process. He no longer saw himself as a victim. He saw her as a gift for his own strength.

Sharon wondered why she stayed with Philip, why she tolerated his brooding hot temper. She looked within and found a mental image of Philip as her villain. She let that pass and found her way into love. As Sharon and Philip freed themselves from negative mental images of one another their true love blossomed.

You never actually feel angry at anyone, only at your disturbing thought of yourself being taken advantage of by that person. You get emotionally hooked into your negative mental images and so aggravate yourself.

Grieving Into Happiness

When things go as you hope they will, you feel a sense of control. But isn't that illusory? Aren't you bound to experience the opposite as well?

You imagine a loss, and so you grieve. You think you grieve over reality? Do you grieve when your lover goes to the store and you anticipate her return in a few minutes? No. You grieve when your lover leaves you for another. In each case, what you expect is sheer illusion.

You imagine grief is worse than joy, and so condemn it and resist it. But grief is the rapid expansion of the heart's capacity for more beauty, love, and joy.

Beyond Betrayal

Do you want more money, more time, more energy, more talent, more joy, more love, more success? Do you wish you looked better? You receive all of this the moment you give up your resistance to the way things are and let go of frightening fantasies of the way you don't want things to be.

Do you feel cheated? The vision of betrayal is all that betrays you. Like its relative jealousy, betrayal projects inferiority onto your experience.

Above Control

When life does not seem under your control, it is *above* your control. To fully appreciate your life, let up on the self-imposed pressure that squeezes out your joy and trust in life.

Pay attention to your thoughts and emotions to see how you create your misery and how to release yourself to joy. This is really all about balance. Balance your power of control with your need to trust in uncontrol. The life you want arrives as you let go of the idea that it has not arrived.

Happiness Works

When you feel happy, you have nothing to worry about. When you feel unhappy, see how you think of yourself and your life. To return to happiness, simply let yourself be, consciously aware of how you feel and what you think. As your awareness deepens and clarifies, so do your peace and joy.

Awareness descends like a pebble cast into a pond. Direct your attention within and it sinks in gradually. As it does, joy's light and lightness spread.

When something tells you that you need something other than what *is* to be happening, look within until you recognize the utterly imaginary nature of your plight. Then watch wisdom guide you with joy.

"No notion have they — not a thought,
That is from joyless regions brought!"
—William Wordsworth

$\mathscr{K}ey\ \mathscr{S}even$

You emotionally react from habit, to the imaginary.

LET'S SAY THAT SOMEONE shows you a kindness, pays you a compliment, or simply casts a smiling gaze your way. How do you react to that, and why? First, you see yourself as favorably as you imagine that person sees you. Then, you automatically react with feelings of approval, appreciation, admiration as you identify with who you imagine yourself to be. It is as if that person's mere *show* of approval gave you permission to finally approve of and forgive *yourself.*

And what occurs next? You worry, "What am I doing right? What is it about me that she likes? Can I do that all the time? *Must I? Do I have to be someone else to preserve this person's approval of who I am?*" In other words you take responsibility for how that person sees you, imagining yourself dependent in some way upon that person's approval. This makes you anxious; so much so that you may even wish that person didn't show any appreciation in the first place.

In the end you have to accept that you do not have what it takes to preserve another's respect. How someone judges you remains beyond your control. The moment you try to prove yourself, you lose yourself.

Life Is Your Solution

Before we realize what we are doing, we react habitually to the imaginary. You imagine you need a person to like you and then you react with anxiety because you cannot make that person like you. Likes and dislikes alternate, like in-breathing and out-breathing. You cannot even know for certain if a person really feels about you the way you think he does.

Awakening to the activity of your imagination determines the difference between living in a problem and living in a solution. Do you relate to your life as a problem or as a solution? Is there something you think you have to do to make your life into what you want it to be, or is your life already automatically what you want it to be? Take a look at your answer: it is purely presumptuous. Then see your tense mode of operating: it is a habitual response to that presumption.

When Opportunity Arrives

When opportunity arrives the fear of missing it or blowing it drives us to feel so anxious that we may wish our opportunity away! All you fear is what you imagine, and your fearful feeling is a habitual reaction to the imaginary.

Some feel so overwhelmed by the responsibility of making the most of their opportunity that they pine for the days before they had it, relishing the simplicity and freedom of less responsibility. And yet, they filled those earlier days with work, longing, and envy for what they now do not value.

It seems that we habitually transform what we have into what we don't want, turning our accomplishments into punishments by imagining life's demands as too much to bear, and responding to that imaginary plight as our reality.

Life Gives You All You Need

Life gives you all you need but habitual emotional reactions to imaginary conditions make you long for something else to be happening. You expect life to work for you while you pit yourself against it. You *think* you are not as well off as you would be if things were different than they are *while you do not really know what is happening.* You punish yourself by identifying with an illusion of your not having or being or doing enough.

Scott felt depressed because he imagined no customers and too little money to cover his expenses. When his friend suggested that he relate with his situation as a solution instead of as a problem, Scott snapped back (as if he had been attacked): "What problem does this situation solve?"

"Where does your problem exist?" asked his friend.

Scott pointed to his surroundings, saying, "Right here. Where are the customers lined up to pay me? Where is the money crossing my palm?"

Scott's friend said, "Look at your thinking. What are you picturing?"

"I'm not picturing anything," Scott retorted.

But over time Scott practiced paying more attention to his thinking, until he saw that he had been unconsciously imagining what he did not want, and emotionally reacting to that imaginary condition as if it was real. During his next conversation with his friend, Scott volunteered, "I may not be able to instantly fill my surroundings with paying customers, but I can control my thinking. And as I let go of thoughts about what I do not want, I experience more peace, more trust, more gratitude, more joy and I see things working out."

Destroy The Competition

Melissa anxiously and resentfully interpreted the actions of a so-called "competitor" as a threat, and she held onto that view as if it shielded her from loss. A friend helped her to see how she beat herself over the head with that "shield." Practicing the discipline of examining her thoughts, Melissa soon realized that she played an incessant mental movie of being outdone by her "competitor". Then she soon discerned that seeing another person in the role of "competitor" was also just an imaginary view, and one that caused her to react with useless demoralization.

"When I let go of the concept of a competitor, I feel myself in a field of limitless abundance," she later shared with her friend. "That keeps me feeling energized and encouraged. In a sense, it destroys the competition."

Do You Imagine
That You Must Not Do What You Want?

Lane felt guilty about doing what she really wanted to do, because she imagined it to be impractical. The longer she put off doing what her heart, her inspiration, her sense of purpose, her feeling of empowerment directed, the more disenchanted with life she became. A friend pointed out that she held back because she held on to a purely imaginary life of dismal demand. Lane finally saw this, chose to take the risk of doing what inspired her, and found peace, power, and profit increasing.

Do you feel plagued by problems of loss, lack, or limitation? What proof do you need to trust that everything is working out wonderfully well for you? That proof arrives as you uncover your habitual mode of fearfully fighting against imaginary danger.

Life Constantly Shows You The Way To Be Free

Take a good look at your present experience of this moment and look for your window of opportunity. It opens through your awareness of your habitual thought and feeling modes that produce your disappointment, frustration, and insecurity. Your freedom automatically follows the moment of your seeing this.

In Your Sleep

In your sleep you dream. You imagine a pointless life. Or you imagine a fearful or meaningless end in death. You imagine your life not working out, your miracle not coming about. You imagine too much wrong with your past. You imagine another's life surpassing yours. You struggle to fix what you are not even sure is broken. And this all happens in the sleep of unconsciousness.

When you look for what you really know about what is going on, the limits of possibility disintegrate before your awakened eyes.

You Attract What You Radiate

How you feel literally fashions your fate, programs life to deliver to you experiences consistent with your feeling state. Live in gloom and attract doom. Turn gloom into glee by letting it be. Let it be in your consciousness and the light sends it scurrying like a rodent seeking the cover of dark it depends upon to exist.

You feel overwrought because you think of a tragic consequence resulting from you not controlling what lies beyond
your calm, sane control. This thought triggers your habitual
pattern of stressful overdrive, but functioning in overdrive creates the chaos you enter the overdrive mode to avoid.

You imagine a depressing future and run it over and over
in your mind, until it consumes your present. You regard
yourself as inadequate in comparison with another. Then, to
compensate, you work so hard you lose the capacity to treat
others kindly. And you expect this strategy to work!

Enter Your Solution Now

You live in the distressing problems that you imagine until
you find the single source of every problem: your imagination
of it. Seeing your thought as only a thought dissolves your
problem's oppressive power over you. This places you in
charge. It frees you to conceive of where you want to go, and
thus to go there.

Problems last as long as you remain attached to the thought
of them. Replaying a problem over and over in your head is an
approach to exiting a problem that gets you deeper into the
problem. It makes you wish that you were dead – and in a
sense you are dead, dead to real life, caught in an imaginary one
that causes you despair.

Change Your Mind

You cannot receive your solution as long as you hold onto
your problem. Every problem is an imaginary condition.
Until you see this, you do not see your mind's projections
upon the screen of reality. Let the thought of your problem
go and you create space for your solution. Your present *is* your
solution. The trick is to stop looking for your solution and to

start looking at it.

Drew felt powerless to improve his life as long as he believed his past choices resulted in his present problem. He examined his mind for a while and shared with his friend this revelation that filled him with the excitement of liberation: "You do not create a present problem through past deeds. You create it through a present thought."

How To Be Problem-Free

On a sheet of paper, write out a description of your most pressing problem. Now, look at that statement and ask yourself, "Where does this problem exist?" You will see that it exists in your mind. Then you will see the fear of letting it go, of letting yourself live in peaceful confidence. This, you will see, is all that traps you in problems.

Now turn your problem into its solution by describing the condition you want in its place. For instance, if your problem is that you smoke, your solution would be that you no longer smoke. Now see where the solution exists and don't imagine yourself out of it.

Remain vigilant of your inner life. Notice the experience generated by your thinking. When thinking places you in a problem, seeing your problem as the sheer mental fabrication it truly is creates space between you and it, space that your solution begins to fill.

Freedom From Your Painful Past

Freedom from your painful past is really just a thought away. Your painful past is a self-punishing illusion that you slavishly re-enter as long as you identify mental fabrication with reality. When you see all memory of the past as a present illusion you release your power to live anew and create a future more in harmony with you.

Forgiveness occurs spontaneously upon your recognition that who you resent is just a figment of your imagination that you have grown attached to. You don't have to live in the hell of the victim and villain another moment. You can free yourself to love.

As long as you hold a grudge, you hold yourself in your painful past. If something you have been wanting in life seems to be held back, consider whom you have left to forgive.

Instead Of Worrying About What Will Happen

Instead of worrying about what will happen do unto yourself as you would have yourself done unto. Your every thought, feeling, spoken word, and action *does* something unto you. Paying closer attention to this automatically leads you into more enjoyable, loving, enlightened living.

Live Beyond Thought Barriers

Thought projects imaginary limits onto your limitless possibility. It creates the one and only barrier between you and who you want to be. Thinking of yourself as *not* creative robs you of your creative potential. Think of yourself as an unhappy person and you make yourself unhappy. Thinking of yourself as weak saps your potential strength. As long as you imagine a division between who you are and who you want to be, you bind yourself to sorrow.

"Woe weeps out her division when she sings."
-Ben Johnson

Key Eight

To escape a frightening situation in a dream, waking up is the way out.

EVERY FRIGHTENING SITUATION in your life is a dream and you can prove this for yourself fairly easily. The next time that you feel anxious or insecure about *anything*, pay closer attention to your mind. You will see that an imaginary scenario frightens you. Every mental vision of your life is the flicker of dream in which you live as long as you hold onto that vision.

You automatically overcome your challenges by waking up to what is really happening, seeing them for what they are. You dig yourself into them more deeply by trying to control a situation that you imagine controlling you.

Troubling Situations

Troubling situations can teach you an invaluable lesson, if you are willing to learn by examining your view of them. Learning your lesson liberates you from the trouble. The lesson has two parts:

1. *You create your disturbing life-scenarios in your mind.*
2. *Believing these scenarios to be outside of you keeps you trapped within them.*

Trouble is life's way of calling upon you to liberate. You cannot imagine how much you have to liberate.

Your Liberation

Your liberation essentially consists of your awakening from the dream of your trouble, awakening to the realization of your trouble being nothing but a dream. You realize you were only dreaming when you wake up from your nightmare. Your liberation from the trouble of your dream then occurs.

Your liberation proceeds as you practice distinguishing between direct conscious experience of you and the purely imaginary idea of you with which you identify when you believe that you're in trouble.

Your idea of yourself trapped, stuck, blocked, denied, or defeated dams your power, turns it against you, delivers your depressing predicaments. Seeing others apparently happy on the outside then leads you to believe them to be better than you are, which makes you feel worse.

Your idea of yourself as less than what your miracle takes, as less than any other person, is nothing but a mental vision that makes it your reality as long as you choose to hold it.

Mental Companions

Any idea that you have of yourself is made of the imaginary "substance" of dream, of illusion. When you think of yourself you view a shimmering phantom-image, a mental hologram, a psychic companion of the real you with which you identify in the sleep of unconsciousness.

This is true about your ideas of others. When you think of someone, when you talk about someone, you view an imaginary construct that you give life to with the power flowing through your belief in it. In the sleep of your unconsciousness you then relate with the person as if the person was that image. In this way you create all of the so-called "difficult" people in your life.

When you feel hurt by someone's mistreatment, you must first interpret the person's behavior to take it in that hurtful way. You *reflect* on how that person mistreated you. You imagine that person's behavior and then feel hurt by *that*. But who is really delivering that mistreatment to you now? You deliver your own thought-blows.

How To Fall In Love

When you fall in love you see nothing wrong. Why? Because you see through the eyes of love, you perceive only beauty. When you feel angry with someone, you see only wrong. Evil enters your interpretation, blotting out innocence.

Living in love is always right for you. There is no healthier, happier, more fulfilled state. When you feel angry, you fall out of happiness and love and into blame. But what are you so angry about? Your own addiction to evil has destroyed the innocence in your heart. Your habit of picturing betrayal has stolen your vision of beauty.

To fall in love with someone is to give you both delight. Here is how to do it: relinquish any idea of that person. Offer that person your direct awareness of your present experience. You'll soon be a conscious agent of love.

Healing Relationships

Joanne called Peter selfish as she complained to a friend about him. "He promised to come see me," she said, "But he decided to stay put when it looked like it would take too much effort to follow through." Joanne then suddenly had an epiphany as she noticed herself picturing a selfish portrayal of Peter. "Why am I choosing to stay with *this?*" she asked herself.

"Exactly," said her friend, who then revealed her own misunderstanding. "You need to drop this guy."

"No," said Joanne. "You don't get me. I'm realizing that how I am *thinking* of Peter needs to be dropped, because that's my way of punishing *me*."

When you recognize a painful scene in your head as a vision, you realize that you take you into that world of pain, and that you do not have to.

Living In No-Past

Practicing this approach to lightening up frees you in so many ways. For instance, it gradually takes you beyond the limits of time, into the eternal present, where you can enter just about any world you choose. The past turns into an illusion of the present, a mirage of a history.

You remain trapped in an inescapable past until this great awakening. Then you see that when you think of a hurtful incident, you hurt yourself by living in that mental vision and in the pain it generates. Seeing this sets you free.

What you have done in the past does not define who you are in the present, though it may foretell your future. You become the person you think of yourself as. Identify yourself with thoughts of yourself as a cruel and selfish person, as a loser, and you give birth to yourself as that person.

When you think of someone hurting you, you enter the

mental world of that person hurting you. You leave the peaceful present for a painful illusion of the past.

Gaining Freedom

Gaining freedom from a painful past that occurred ten minutes ago or ten years ago happens as you look within to see where that so-called "past event" actually exists. Then you see how you conjure it up with a present thought and how you needlessly trouble yourself with that thought

You see, for instance, that *thinking* about how someone related to you in a manner that left you feeling demeaned *makes you feel demeaned right now*. You see now that you only *thought* you had to change that person's view of you to regain your self-respect. You see now that it is your own vision of yourself that you have to change by simply letting go of it. This frees you from feeling overpowered by another person.

Paying attention to your present experience places you on your happy, loving path through life. Mentally holding onto hurtful events blinds you to that path and binds you to despair. For instance, until you pay close attention to your thinking, you think that holding onto an idea of a person's past betrayal of your trust protects you from further loss, while it actually recreates that loss.

Who Is He Now?

Who is he now, that person who seemed to be selfish or cruel or intimidating or unreliable in your past? To be honest and truthful, you have to admit that all of your "villains" are just ideas that you entertain. We find the unknown so uncomfortable that we choose to live in the illusion of certainty, even when what we feel certain about frightens, frustrates, and depresses us.

Those who live in the past live in their ideas; remaining dead to their present, they miss their present opportunities.

Your oppressive limitations exist only in your thought of them, and your awareness of their sheer thought-basis sweeps them away. You need no idea of what is, was, or will be happening to find happiness.

Awaken From Memory

I recently had a conversation with a friend who could not accept the fact that the past is an illusion. Perhaps I will have better luck with you.

Remember something now. Perhaps you recall what you ate for breakfast. Where does that scene exist? Right. It exists in your head. Remember something painful and you go into a dream where you re-experience the pain as long as the dream lasts.

When you look at what you really know, and become aware of the presumptions you have surrounding everything, then you realize that all you know is occurring in its present form of existence.

You cannot fix who you are by identifying with who you were. You cannot fix another person by identifying that person with your memory of what she did wrong. You cannot change your life by holding onto an idea of the life you want to leave.

Do You Think Against Yourself?

As long you see yourself as you *were* you feel lost, constrained, and oppressed - blocked from growing, not free. As long as you relate with another person who identifies you with his mental image of you, you feel like you do not really exist in that relationship. That person's vision of you exerts a restrictive force that makes you feel boxed in, trapped, powerless.

You may think of your spouse or your child, a dog or the weather doing something against you, but that merely expresses a way that you *think* against yourself.

You do to you in the present whatever you remember being done to you. You enter the experience that you think of. Seeing this frees you from the illusory power the experience held over you. It wakes you up to a whole new world of freedom, including the freedom for your miracle to be. Nothing holds you back when you let go of the idea that anything can hold you back.

To Be A Happy Person

Thinking of past evils done unto you makes you their victim in the present. Thinking of people mistreating you makes no more sense than choosing to spend time with someone who mistreats you. As long as you associate with a *mental companion* who takes advantage of you, you leave no space for loving care to come your way.

Who you think you are is one of your mental companions. Do you think of yourself as unhappy? You become the unhappy person that you remind yourself that you are. Your freedom to be happy lies in your power to let go of the idea of yourself as unhappy.

10 Points To Light Your Way

- People who distrust you actually distrust an illusion they cling to for a false sense of control.
- The energy you expend in holding onto imaginary problems costs you the energy you need to awaken to present solutions.
- The person you were is nothing but an idea held in the mind of the person you are.
- If you can think about it or talk about it, it is not really happening now.
- The next time that you feel less than completely happy

look within for the vision of yourself in an unhappy state with which you identify.

- Let the unknown ignite your drive to give your very best to this moment, to make the most of it, to fully appreciate your total freedom now.
- When you feel deserted by others, by life, by God see how you are actually deserting yourself by living in the idea of that desertion.
- Any idea of who you are is not you, but a form of imaginary substance beheld by the idea viewer. Return to your true self by dis-identifying yourself with any idea's representation.
- All you love returns to you in the miracle of your awakening from the illusion of your separation from all you love.
- Your past ends when you enter the present.

"The mind is its own place,
and in itself Can make a Heaven
of Hell, a Hell of Heaven."
—John Milton

Key Nine

Revisit your hometown for a departure from past limits.

RETURNING TO PLACES in which you spent significant time can assist your disencumberment from dark patterns that return you to what feels like a never-ending defeat. The place where you were brought up brings up the roots of habitual mindsets that bring you down to this day. These may include a depressing belief in your inadequacy that has been subconsciously pounding you ever since.

As you walk through the streets of your old neighborhood, notice the old, familiar thoughts that turn your spirit to lead. These might include ideas of yourself as weak and incompetent, dependent, unworthy of love and respect that you first bought into there. As you now consciously observe your thoughts, you can see them as the mere ideas they always were, and so at last make real headway in your liberation.

See What Familiar Faces Stir Up

You can accomplish something similar by revisiting people from your past. While reuniting with one of your relatives or old chums, face your *internal* experience to free yourself at the core from your underlying feelings of insecurity, resentment, inferiority. Witness yourself acting out an old, helpless role, or wearing an equally false know-it-all disguise, that really isn't you, never really was you, but which set the stage for you to lose yourself ever since.

The Gift Of Difficult Situations

The gift of difficult situations abides in their invitation. They invite you to see the destructive reaction patterns lying beneath the surface of your awareness, embedded in your subconscious in another time and place, just waiting for their opportunity to spring their dark magic on you. Whether you are spending time with a cantankerous relative who will not see you as you are, or facing a challenge that mismatches your expectations of a successful life, the thought of yourself as inadequate is all that makes you experience inadequacy. As you awaken to the level of consciousness beyond your thinking, you automatically withdraw all power from self-sabotaging mindsets.

A Miracle Invasion

We can define a miracle as an occurrence of something too wonderful to completely believe in. A miracle pauses against the resistance of your depressing anticipation. You live in the world you believe you're in. When you feel stormed by dark chaos, threatened by trouble, disheartened by let down, it is your bright miracle crashing against the wall of your resistance. The experience you most frightfully resist contains the miracle for which you most solemnly pray.

The Miracle Mindset

The miracle mindset transforms your walls into open doors to the miracle in life that you want to be yours. The miracle mindset becomes yours as you pay closer attention to the depressing and frightening anticipations and interpretations that deny your miracle now. This erases the dark vision that obscured the mysterious and sentenced you to the gloom of imaginary doom.

You Experience A Miracle

You experience a miracle, *your* miracle, the one you want with all your heart, all the time – right now in fact. Your miracle happens when something happens to you that feels too wrong to be right and too good to be true. You experience a miracle when life makes no sense. A miracle blasts reason to smithereens.

Let's say that you want a particular job and feel crestfallen when the opportunity for that job falls through. You examine how your mind deals with this and witness fearful anticipations, painful memories, and depressing interpretations. You see them as the illusions they are and realize that you really don't know what this means. Then you find you can open your heart and mind to the vision of faith, and your disappointment turns out to be your miracle's onset.

You Will Lose Everything But Your Miracle

You are only at home in your miracle. The miraculous is your origin as well as your destination. Your whole life is a miracle. *You* are one. You must lose all you feel attached to and dependent upon to see that you are always intact, always supported, always free. The arrival of what you do not want offers you the most direct way to all you desire. You experience a miracle when you fall in love; though falling in love seems to happen at the wrong time, falling in love actually *rights* time.

All is forgiven when you enter your miracle. No one can take anything from you, but your thought of them doing so takes it from you.

The Opposite Of A Miracle Mindset

The opposite of a miracle mindset is "the depression mindset". We live in its deadening blandness when we confuse direct conscious experience with our boring notions. This drab mindset creates illusory abandonment. It makes everything *but* the miraculous seem real. We have fallen under its spell when we believe that life or love can ever be wrong.

Until you see your love-starved, no-miracle life as imaginary, you mistake pessimism for realism.

Sometimes we try to believe in our miracle through positive thinking, but this inevitably fails because you cannot keep your thoughts up, no more than you can keep your hand up indefinitely. Faith returns in the absence of a negative thought – while holding onto a positive one may only cover up an underlying negative one. A miracle mindset takes no thought at all. Then you can *see* your miracle actually happening.

The Control That You Have

Positive thinking works, but only to a degree. When you feel inspired and free, focus on what you want. When you start feeling low, though, just observe your thoughts to clear your mind of fear's lies. Alternate like that: think positive from inspiration, and purge from desperation.

Take action for what you want. Persevere. Let every situation teach you how to go through it. This defines your way to any goal. But to be *in* your destination you must exchange striving for arriving. You can bring yourself right up to the brink of all you want, but you cannot step into it. You have to accept it.

You Are A Miracle Receiver

Thinking can be wrong but reality is always right. Let that be a lesson to you. You never know where reality leads, though you think your way into desperation. You might believe that someone has betrayed your trust. Nevertheless, everyone gives you just what you need to grow into your limitless potential of a miracle receiving station. So even betrayal, on the level of appearance and logic, equals perfectly loving faithfulness on a deeper level, in truth.

Life Is Perfectly Designed

Life is perfectly designed to trigger your fear and depression so you can let both go, which lets you go into your miracle. You cannot release what you do not know that you hold onto.

You might imagine that your miracle life is not worth all the pain that life heaps on you. Can you now finally see how that view is entirely illusory?

Facing your deepest depression and gravest fear sets you free of believing in their illusory basis. So those terrible trials that you resist come to bless you, to release you from their false clutches.

When you feel depressed or insecure ask yourself, "What unhappy possibility am I predicting?" Then, look within, at your mind. Frightening, depressing dramas of the mind masquerades as reality at a deep, subtle level not always quickly discerned. Even before you see the cause, just looking within begins the eviction process that dislodges you from your frightening and depressing dilemmas.

Assault Of Inadequacy

After receiving a shocking rejection from her boyfriend of three years, Linda felt like she was drowning in a deluge of brokenhearted fears. But she courageously explored the full torrent of her reaction and passed through a thousand memories that battered her with beliefs in her inadequacy. Her body literally writhed in agony as she consciously descended into the core of an experience she could only describe as her quintessential unworthiness. But after relentlessly viewing her total feeling of total failing, she gradually awoke into a most sacred peace at the very ground of her true being. She had purged a deadly attitude of self-criticism that had been lodged in the depths of her subconscious, plaguing her nearly all of her life.

From that point forward her life steadily transformed into the glorious miracle she had always hoped it could be.

The Loss Of Our Illusions

We are better off facing head-on the painful feelings we harbor and would rather run away from. Facing aching feelings such as unworthiness, insecurity, dependency, and even hate discharges their power over you.

Feelings of depression, frustration, and insecurity signal that you live in the illusion of life and love not working out. Like poison mushrooms mental illusions thrive in the dark, in the darkness of your unconscious. In the light of awareness they turn out to be empty halucinations.

Your Miracle Dawns

What do you imagine is really going on in your life now? What do you imagine your past was really all about? What do you imagine happening next, in your immediate and long-term future? Are you in hell? Are you in heaven? Are you actually living through all of this or really seeing your life flash before your eyes in your passing? Are you already dead and *this* is your after-life? Are you sleeping? Is any loss really a loss? Or is it really gain? Can anyone really be better off than you? Do you really have anything to worry about? To face the truth is to have to admit that you really do not know.

When you honestly face the unknown, you cannot worry or feel depressed. You get worried and depressed over the imaginary nightmare visions you project onto the unknown. The longer you pay close attention to your mind, the more its frightening and depressing ideas fade into the dawning light of your endless miracle.

We Remain Lost In Our Illusions

We remain lost in our illusions until we see them *as* illusions. You think yourself into the pain of feeling that you are not good enough until you see that you are not your thought of you. It takes very sharp awareness to recognize what you actually think of yourself, and sharper awareness still to discern that as just a thought. Your awareness sharpens through the practice of focusing attention within, looking for the inner source of your present experience.

Too much indulgence in nicotine and other drugs and alcohol, too much rushing around, too much chatter about nothing, too much mindless TV viewing dulls the consciousness and enslaves it to illusion.

Whoever Controls Your Illusions Controls You

When you control your mental illusions, you control your life, because you bring about what you think about. You can envision what you choose and, in so doing, choose your fate.

But when you do not recognize the illusory nature of your mental experiences, you leave yourself vulnerable to manipulation by others. Weak minded, dim-witted masses fall prey to manipulative thought-mongers. A common trick is to accuse others of doing what they themselves are guilty of. When you say "they" or "him" or "her" in your accusations, hear "I".

You Painfully Believe

You painfully believe that you are angry at the person that you feel angry at until you see that you feel angry at an imaginary version of that person that you view in your mind. You think that you are right and that someone else is wrong until you see that you look at an idea of that person in the wrong to hide your own self-doubt. You painfully worry that you are in a bad situation until you see that you imagine a bad situation and merely *think* yourself into it.

Unconsciously dwelling in what you dread materializes it. That is why life appears to be consistent with your fears. Believing in depressing concepts produces disappointing results. This makes you feel mysteriously stuck. You painfully regret what you did in your past until you see that you create that past in your present through the mental scenario you regret.

Enter The Field Of No-Answer

"Why did so-and-so have to die?" "Why did so-and-so have to lie to me and leave?" We seek right answers from wrong questions. The right question is, "How am I presently giving myself what I am experiencing?" There really is no going back. Nothing is as it was. For all we know, nothing ever really was.

"It is foolish presumption to go around disdaining and condemning as false whatever does not seem likely to us."
-Michel de Montaigne

Key Ten

Are you looking for a way out?
The way is in!

HERE IS AN INSIGHT for getting out of *any* undesired situation: your struggle to get out keeps you in... your struggle! Observe the condition you wish to exit until you see your mind's projection of it upon your limitless present. As long as you fear it, you conceive of it. When you let fear pass through you, what you fear loses its hold on you!

Freedom takes over when you let yourself be. Quietly observe your mind to see you're imagining yourself into wherever you want out of. As long as you go on figuring out why you need to get out you figure yourself in. The way out is to let your thought of it out, let it go out to wherever thought vanishes to.

The Adventure In

You feel trapped in an abusive relationship with life or with another person because your frightful fight to take flight keeps you stuck in your plight. To leave the abuse, leave the self-abuse of imagining your abuser. Examine your thoughts to see the imaginary world in which your adversary opposes your interests, and see further that he, she, them, or it exists nowhere else.

Going within takes you on an adventure in which you get to really play the hero who releases the one in distress (you) and returns home with the golden prize beyond price (awakened consciousness).

Brady felt trapped in life's flatness. He feared looking back at the end of his life with the regret of one who never really lived. When he heard of someone else's exciting adventure, like rafting down the Amazon or hiking up the Alps, he felt more stuck in limitation, loss, and lack. Then he saw how his imagination produced his disappointment, that he merely *imagined* others in an adventure and himself out of one. This turned his life into an adventure of boundless possibility.

Enter Suffering

Angelina feared that her suffering would last forever. As she began examining her unhappiness instead of resisting it, she learned: "My idea of forever is just a thought. Thinking of endless suffering expands my suffering. Infusing awareness with suffering makes me wiser, stronger, spiritually deeper, more loving and altogether freer. My resistance to suffering serves only to increase it."

Wisdom Whispers Softly In The Inner Space Of Silence

Wisdom enters as you enter conscious observation of your present experience. Wisdom leaves when you allow any experience to swallow up your awareness. Wisdom and joy unite, with peace and love, as eternal companions.

To make the right decision, do not live in your ideas of what will happen if you do this or that. Just observe your present experience of concern and you will know exactly what to do. Awareness of what is happening takes you above what is happening, raising your life to a higher level.

You gain wisdom by studying the relationship between your choices and what happens to you. For instance, you can observe that when you imagine what you do not want you feel depressed. But you feel depressed only over the way you *think* things are. You feel depressed over a mental movie that you get caught up in. The movie ends when you see the credits, when you see that you are the producer.

Shackled By A Miracle

Margaret was a new mom. At first this was her miracle, but to her shock and dismay she soon felt depressed because motherhood meant confinement. This turned into resentment toward her child and her husband.

Examining her pain revealed her imagination to be the source of her unhappiness. "Where did I learn to think this way?" she wondered. Her answer came with some surprise. "This is how my mother thought and felt! I have been repeating *her* parenting pattern." The painful wound of the life-long strife between Margaret and her own mother healed in the light of this understanding, the wound aggravated by her own motherhood. This released her to return to her sacred love for her child, her husband, and her miracle life.

Enter Conflict

The way out of conflict is also the way in. Conflict exists as a state of mind only. You have to think of opposition to enter strife.

Fred felt conflicted about his job. He wanted out but felt too dependent upon the paycheck. He sought escape from his belief in his cowardice by blaming his wife and children. He began drinking every night for numbness only to find out that even when you think you lost all of your self-respect you can always find more to lose.

At last, instead of beating himself up for not getting out, he went into his experience with more conscious awareness and drew out more and more delight. His wife noticed the dramatic change and inquired of its source. "I looked within and found myself," he said with a grin not made of gin, "as free as I am from a thought."

Shift Your Focus

Alice, a successful but unhappy motion picture screenwriter, wanted out of her marital conflict. She thought incessantly of the bickering and worried nervously about the ill effects it had on her two young children. When she shifted the focus of her attention from seeing no way out to seeing what she imagined herself in, the situation dramatically shifted. She learned that recognizing a mental movie as a mental movie lets you write the script of your life.

Awaken To Freedom From Dark Inner Habits

It takes disciplined work to build up the strength of any new habit, including the habit of looking within for the source of unhappiness. Destructive inner habits take time and effort to lose.

Burns worried that he would never amount to anything until he saw that as just living in an imaginary box. The more he deliberately lived in conscious examination of his inner experience, the more he experienced the absence of barriers to fulfilling a great cause.

Ken saw through self-observation that since childhood he had fed and nurtured the habit of feeling alienated, isolated, abandoned, and alone. By channeling his energy into practice of the habit of looking within, he drained the power out of the habit of dwelling in the drama of lonely isolation and discovered growing fulfillment in relationships.

You enter bright reality by seeing all frightening scenarios as fantasies of reality turned against you.

A Gift Of Devastation

William felt devastated when his fiancé left him six days before their gala wedding. Relentlessly facing every ounce of his humiliating pain gradually revealed the healing light, and he saw that his pain came from imagining himself unworthy and his life without love. Slowly this released him from dark, inner projection and his anxiety and depression dissolved into the astounding awareness of a limitless new life.

"The deeper your devastation," he later said to a friend, "the greater your opportunity to get free from the shackles of fear and depression that otherwise limit your life."

When you feel unhappy, anxious or angry, look within to see how:

- *Your frustrating sense of being stuck places you in the frustrated sense of being stuck.*
- *Your angry reaction sends you into your anger and the circumstances that trigger it.*
- *Your feelings of dissatisfaction plunge you into flat, unful-*

filling experience.
- *Your impatient reaction delivers to you the maddening sense of endless delay.*
- *Your anxiety and insecurity make life look threatening.*
- *Your hopelessness dooms you to despair.*

Fear Is A Fraud

Fear tries to sell you on something going wrong in your life, while your life is working out fine - better than fine... *miraculously!* You have nothing to worry about, but worry drives you into what you fear. All you fear is a contrived life-scenario of lack playing like a movie in your head.

Depression is another fraud. It tells you that your miracle is not present. What makes you think your life lacks any luster right now? Your mind makes you think it. Only an idea portrays your life as anything less than the answer to your deepest prayers.

Sarah felt depressed because her mate no longer appeared to be the man she had hoped to end up with. It took her a while of looking at her mind to see that her disappointment lasted only as long as she chose to live in disappointment-producing thought.

In Real Life We Are All Free

When you experience any sense of inadequacy happening in your life you live in a mental projection of inadequacy that blinds you to the miraculous. Since you manifest the experience you enter within, the more you want out the more you dig in.

When you feel envious, you enter an imaginary world in which someone else's life is superior to your own and something is lacking in yours. This is a way you rob yourself of your miracle.

See how anxious suspicion works similarly. You imagine someone betraying your trust and lose your self-respect. Each time that you relive that thought you get taken advantage of again.

Instead of looking at why your misery is justified, see how it is a response to a dream.

Trust

To experience happiness and success requires nothing more than trust in life. Entrust yourself to life rather than to a mental movie of yourself deprived. Your real life frees you from unhappiness and failure as you recognize when you live in the inner vision of a life that you don't want.

When something went wrong during a film shoot, Larry worried that it will be too hard to fix and will cause irreparable harm to his career as a cinematographer. Upon looking within, he came to see that he exchanged trust for anxiety by entering an imaginary consequence of greater disappointment. Seeing this began his release from his pointless prison of pain. Larry learned this lesson: "To enter trust you do not need to imagine how things can be working out in your favor. Trust is the natural state of living in awareness without a negative thought."

Everything always works out in reality.

Strengthen Your Inner Light

You either continue moving forward or you begin falling back. But even falling back, when done consciously, turns into forward movement. Leslie lost a painting she had worked on for a year. It went up in a blaze in an art gallery fire. She examined her inner experience until she discerned the imaginary from the real. "All I lost has set me free," she said. "Free to live beyond the false limits of mere mental destiny."

Working through each wave of inner darkness brings about the dawning of brighter, stronger inner light. Every let down equals a step up.

Your habit of dwelling in hopelessness is all that holds you in its lair. Each time you work your way through it, you let the darkness of hopelessness strengthen your light of joyful expectation.

Greater Happiness Is On The Way

When you receive what you do not want, you receive the opportunity you need to bring what you do want about. You enter disappointment, though, by living in the illusion of a situation you do not want. Anything that you imagine is already yours. A miracle is contingent only upon your acceptance of it. To look down on your life is to send yourself into a lower life.

When something so painful happens that you cannot imagine how it can be good for you, stop relying on your ability to figure things out. When you cannot figure out how to make something work out, it's time to leave your thinking mind behind. Faith proves itself in time. Your life continually invites you into greater happiness, whether you want to move on or not. Those events that send you into unhappy, insecure conditions reveal how to free yourself from them.

*"Don't worry about those dreams none,
they're only in your head."*
-Bob Dylan

Key Eleven

Your imaginary dependence keeps you in dependence.

YOU CAN BE INDEPENDENT or in dependence. Dependence is an imaginary condition, a dream. You lose that dream when you wake up.

But it hurts to lose a dream, because hope lives on dreams. You imagine your life working out living in a particular kind of area, with a particular person, in a particular relationship, achieving a particular level in your career, making a particular income. When that particular dream appears to be impossible, you feel crestfallen *because you can't imagine your life working out.*

But you really don't have to. Deeper than the dream of imagining your life not working is the dream that you have to imagine it working for it to work!

Whatever or whomever you think you need to be happy

will not make you happy in any lasting way, while your belief in that need keeps you miserable.

Imagining that your fulfillment depends upon any particular outcome fabricates a reality that grips you in fear. You imagine a reality that can *not* work. This repels the very condition you desire.

Unrequited Love

We call a relationship in which you want someone who retreats from you, "unrequited love". You can be in that sort of relationship with money, with a career, with a waistline. And in this relationship you remain until you awaken from the enchantment of wanting.

Accepting all people, all experiences as equal transforms the longing of a dissatisfied life of unrequited love into true, boundless fulfillment.

Living in the emptiness of desire, mining the experience of it for all that it is worth, frees you from the pit of it.

Requited Love

When you let your life flow it goes the way you want it to, a demonstration of the power of faith. But you must uncover your underlying feeling of need, always based on fear, to *let* life pull you through, into your greatest miracle yet.

Grasping freezes you into a state of internal vacancy and draws you into a future of old longings and resentments. Let hopes pass, bid them adieu, and accept the peace that you would love to happen now.

James lost money on a bold investment. He sorely wished he hadn't, until he looked within. There he observed his prediction of life's punishment: his financial ruin. Then he realized that punishment was self-inflicted by his thought of it, and this helped him let it go. He looked at what he gained, and the wisdom pointed to riches.

Let Go Of Your Losses To Receive Your Gains

We hold onto a loss because we fear the cost. But trust in life makes our so-called "errors" free. What if you *knew* that a mistake, a loss, a let down imposed no real cost upon you? Why imagine a need to be rescued? Your life has only one direction: from the miraculous, through the miraculous, to the miraculous.

"No one should have to suffer this much," Judi said after she felt robbed of love by life. "God must be a sadist, if there *is* a God," she sobbed on to a friend. "And I know this is the wrong way to feel."

Her friend suggested that she examine her experience, including her experience of judging herself. Judi felt so emptied of wisdom that she took this plunge and eventually emerged with this wisdom: "Don't resist your true feelings. Just observe them. See how thought generates your frightened, depressing, angry mourning. Just be honest with yourself to emerge whole from the ruins of your broken dream."

You Have Everything To Feel Grateful For

See how gratitude shapes experience. Make the shift out of depressing illusion by expressing gratitude for *all* that you experience, including the suffering and the loss. Relate to whatever happens as the opening of your miracle. You don't have to know how what is can work for you. When you choose gratitude, you lose the barrier to your miracle.

Look back at the painful and pleasant episodes of your past and say, "Thank you" to each one. This opens your subconscious to accept the infinite good. Look at your present experience and express gratitude for it. Gratitude opens your heart to love. Don't wait for your logical mind to give you a reason to feel grateful. Be grateful first. That is how you lead your logical mind to gratitude-supporting reasons.

Here Is Your Gift

In what area of life do you feel stuck? Try shifting from resistance, into gratitude. Try shifting from the perspective that sees your present as a curse, to one that relates to it as a blessing. Try relating to it as a gift instead of as a loss. This is an exercise that develops your inner strength over time, your strength to see the good, the gift, the blessing, the miracle being presented to you now.

"But I see nothing to feel grateful about," said Paul, when he heard this.

"Try being grateful anyway," Paul's friend advised. Paul worked at it for a while. The first gem he came up with was this: "I can see no reason not to keep grateful."

Give yourself permission to live in the appreciation of *everything* that happens. Affirm: I am totally grateful for my present situation.

A Lie

A lie is perpetrated for the false sense of power it provides its user. The person who spews out venomous blame, harsh and unforgiving criticism and vitriolic condemnation insinuates the lie that others are the way he chooses to portray them. But forgiveness is automatic when you see how you create what you condemn.

We lie to ourselves with every depressing, frightening possibility that we entertain. We would rather believe that life can let us down then admit to ourselves that we really do not know what is going on. Why? We attach shame to not knowing. Believing in the lie that tells us we are supposed to know, we pretend to.

We lie to win in relationships, but the truth is that we attract people like ourselves. Liars attract liars. The more you lie the more you count on liars to be honest with you. To be honest with yourself, you have to admit that you do not know that your miracle is not happening now.

The Dawning Of Creation

Look within until you wake up to the panoply of dark images that parade with grim menace before your mind's inner eye. This includes your frightening, frustrating, and depressing visions of your life, yourself, and other people. I call this awakening "*The Dawning of Creation*" because you see in its flash how you create the make-believe universe that you don't want to live in and discover your open door to God's Creation: a world without any form of impoverishment, deprivation, or disadvantage.

An Enlightening Exercise

On a length of string, tie 18 knots (remember what 18 means?) about an inch apart. When you lie down for sleep at the close of the day, hold the string between your thumb and index finger. Close your eyes and observe your thoughts. Each time a thought enters your mind, pull the string to one of the knots. Pressing the knot between your two fingers, state silently to that thought, "You are just a thought."

Continue this exercise until you reach the last knot or until you drift off to sleep before reaching the end. After just a few nights of this practice you will find yourself freer from the tyranny of your dark-thinking mind.

You Leave What You Seek

The more you want to get, the more want you get. Do you want to get finished with some project, task, or trial? What do you give yourself by going into that? Do you want to get more money, more cooperation, more approval, more free time, more autonomy, more credit, more understanding? Only as long as you imagine yourself without.

Bickering couples have this to learn. When you let go of the mere notion that tells you that you need more from your mate than he or she willingly gives, you find all you want.

That for which you desperately seek incessantly retreats because your desperation generates your division from fulfillment. In desperation, you struggle to avoid loss by living in it.

Wise Waiting

Waiting wisely ends waiting, turns a let down into a lift off. It eliminates the illusion of time's division. When you think you have to wait, observe *how* you wait. When your mind portrays where you are as a waste you enter that waste. Seeing your idea of being stalled as just an idea delivers you from delay's limitations and losses.

The hardest waiting comes during the severe pain of a love's loss, the pain that feels like agony every moment, and even inner death. It can take *years* to pass through that pain. But even that is nothing to wait for, nothing to look forward to. Life's deepest secrets and most sacred treasures are buried in your deepest losses. The longer and lower you dig down, the more the springboard of life builds up its spring to launch you into your highest miracle.

You Create Your Wait

You never actually have to wait. You can produce every moment. When you think you have to wait, observe what you make of each moment until you see how you make it pleasant or painful. This lifts the weight of wait; it turns it into an enlightening lesson in wise living.

Time is only "something" you imagine behind and before you. It is, therefore, illusion. When you live in the present, you have reached the end of time. Plant the seeds of loving, intelligent action aimed at the results you intend and those seeds bloom into the destiny you desire. How long *must* you wait? *No* time. Do all you can for all you want right now, without a thought that places you under the imaginary pressure of time. Only a thought places time between you and your desire. Impatience pits you against a non-existent adversity.

Now Delivers

Now delivers your present opportunity. The better you receive it, the richer your harvest. The present invites you to make the delightful discovery that you have nothing to wait for when you stop putting off your life. Look for all you want from this moment and find the miraculous now. Patience, or the art of living without time-pressure, releases you from the painful illusion that what you want is locked up in a distant future. When you feel the pressure of impatience, see *impatience* as a waste of time.

Patience

To be patient, work *with* life instead of against life. Stop rejecting the way things are before you fully explore that way. Patience frees you from dependency on what is not, reveals the infinite worth of what is. Patience opens your door to infinite fulfillment. The patient attend this moment fully and let this moment attend to them.

Humility

You are humbled or humiliated. Life removes dependencies, proving that you cannot even depend upon yourself. Awareness reveals that you don't have to.

Sue found herself groveling at the bottom of a fall from grace that she never imagined possible. Before she learned that an encounter with the impossible begins the miraculous, she felt the worst loss – the loss of faith in herself. There, in that loathsome, naked space, she found her freedom by facing herself until she saw that what at first seemed like ultimate self-disclosure turned out to be nothing but a deeply crafted illusion. She discovered then and there that she does not have to depend upon herself when nothing but the imaginary goes wrong. This turned her fall upside down.

The Price You Have To Pay

The price you have to pay for all you really want is facing the fiction you don't want. You want freedom from dependency most of all, because that equals freedom from fear.

When you don't have what you need to prop up your arrogance, just let yourself be. You seek proof of your superiority as long as you believe in your inferiority.

When you feel humiliated, you humiliate yourself with the idea of yourself as disgraced.

Humiliation greets the ungrateful. Humility and gratitude go together. While your haughty mind finds fault, if you fully appreciate the total gift of this moment you cannot help but feel humbled by the grace of God.

"The mind is much, but is not all."
-Lord Byron

Key Twelve

You receive the compassion
that you give.

THE ATTITUDE YOU EXPRESS toward another is an experience you deliver to yourself. You can only share the feeling that you hold onto. Thus, you treat yourself the way you treat others and you treat others the way you treat yourself. You treat yourself as worthy of love to the degree that you live in love.

Living in love does not require others to change. It requires your trust in love.

Self-Accusation

When you accuse another you direct the assault of accusation toward yourself. In other words, you treat yourself as one deserving of the blame. You beat yourself up over someone letting you down.

When you feel frustrated by another's behavior, take that as a sign that you need to lighten up *on yourself.* Resentfully blaming another delivers a brutal attack upon yourself.

You Waste Your Effort

You waste your effort trying to make others treat you better while mistreating yourself. Complaining conveys a condescending, harshly critical attitude that you deliver to yourself. You cannot help feeling betrayed as long as you continue living in the experience of betrayal. When you see your attitude toward others as a way of treating yourself, you find the key to freedom that is love.

The Way You Live

The way you live is exactly how you treat yourself. Are you looking at how you treat yourself right now or are you distracted by how you imagine others behaving, or by how you imagine life to be treating you?

The better you treat yourself, the better life you lead. To receive the best life has to offer, treat yourself as well as you possibly can. Observe the impact of your choices upon you. How you live in the present defines your fate.

When you do not see how you treat you, you fall for the illusion of some outside source of mistreatment and create an inadequate life to live in. This makes you feel trapped in problems that seem overpowering.

The Fall Of Superiority

Thinking of any person or condition as superior has the same destructive effect as thinking of any person or condition as inferior. To think of a superior you have to conceive of an inferior. This gives you what you don't want. In other words, you occupy the condition you look down upon. (This traps all big-ots. Holding onto their idea of "the other's" inferiority imprisons them in the condition they hate.)

When you believe that your view of a person or condition equals that person or condition you cannot get away from where you do not want to be. But when you see your view as just a scene in your head, you can let it go before it brings you down. When you feel condemnation toward any person, situation, or experience you condemn yourself to a world where love does not exist.

Awaken To The Inner Dynamics

Awaken to the inner dynamics of self-attack to release yourself from the damaging onslaught of self-deprecating beliefs. When someone does not come through for you, when life does not come through for you, see how well your view comes through for you. Your thought of yourself, of another, of what happened to you, or of what is happening to you, is what *you are doing to you.*

The Secret Solution

You no longer suffer the plight of a victim when you release your oppressing notions that make you feel like a victim. When you feel taken advantage of, bullied, or mistreated in any way, take a quick look at your present way of treating yourself. You attack yourself with condemnation and hold yourself in the position that you do not want to be in.

No one is the person you believe him or her to be. *You* are also beyond belief. So is your life!

You don't want any more problems, do you? Yet, you give yourself every problem you have. You have to think about your problem to remember that you have a problem. Instead of fret-

ting about how to get out of the problems that you think yourself in, stop thinking yourself into them. Therein lies your secret
solution to *all* problems.

Build A New Habit

Does your idea of who you are, of who you were, of who
you will be work for you or against you? Does it imprison or
liberate you? Does it beat you down or let you up?

How you see yourself is a way you treat yourself, and it
comes from mere habitual thinking. If you have spent years
thinking of yourself as inferior, inadequate, insignificant, inca-
pable or your life as below your standards for self-respect, the
habit cuts you deeply and it will take time to leave. The sooner you begin shedding light within, the sooner depressing,
degrading views of yourself depart, setting you free to fulfill
your greater destiny.

Don't waste effort condemning yourself for condemning
yourself. Simply develop the new habit of looking within.
The exercise of looking within builds strength and depth in
your perception. Soon you see that what you think of yourself is a way of treating yourself. This releases you to love.

Your Way

Treat yourself to your true way of happy success by engag-
ing in what inspires you. Feed your soul with inspiration. Pay
very close attention to how you live in this moment in order
to find the way that inspires you. You are either inspiring or
expiring your spirit. The next time that you feel disappointed
just do something that you love. Give yourself that now.

When you do not know what to do, trusting that you do
not have to know sets you free. You worry that you are not
doing enough, that you do not know enough, that you do not

have enough, that you *are* not enough. But this is just a habit.

Pay attention to your angry, critical responses. See how *they* torment you, not the conditions at which you direct them.

Let Go Of Your Inner Tormentor

What you think of yourself manifests a life consistent with that self, *whether you think it consciously or unconsciously.* Your self-tormenting idea of yourself as a failure attracts disappointment and makes your circumstances match your idea of failure. Drop your angry thoughts of yourself to set your success-filled destiny free.

When you feel insecure, pressured, frustrated, tense, nervous, blocked you gravitate toward conditions that support those feelings. While habitually reporting to yourself that you are not good enough, smart enough, strong enough, responsible enough, talented enough, beautiful enough your dissatisfying achievements will prove you right.

Release Yourself From Self-Punishing Ideas

Release yourself from self-punishing ideas to discover that you always were, are, and will be *more* than adequate to meet all of life's challenges and to achieve all that you desire. Do this to know that this holds true for everyone in the world, to know that you have no one to look up to, no one to look down upon, and nothing at all to denigrate. I am not asking you to believe in such exhilarating notions. I only suggest that you release the unfounded beliefs that place you in a lower world where you mistreat yourself.

Life Answers Your Prayers

Direct attention within to witness the incessant stream of mental and emotional self-assault troubling you nearly all the time. You will soon see how you have been unconsciously mistreating yourself and blaming it on life.

Life tells you the story of your miracles but you drown it out by telling yourself a story of sad disappointment, disaster, and disgrace. You cannot imagine the full scope of power, freedom, beauty, and brilliant magnificence available to you now. The moment you imagine yourself, other people, or the world as less than all you long to be, you miss life's answers to your deepest prayers.

Release Your Beautiful Magnificence

Release your beautiful magnificence by dropping depressing ideas of yourself. Instead of blaming yourself for a life you don't want, let go of that life and the self who perpetuates it. Here is how.

Think of something you did in your past that you feel disturbed about. Notice how you react to that thought. You might call yourself a jerk. You feel stabs of emotional pain. You feel trapped in what you did, powerless to get out of it, powerless to make it so that it never happened. But weren't you out of it the moment before you thought of it?

Observe what is happening within you. Make your inner experience conscious. Keep looking at how you think and feel until you see how *your reactions keep you stuck in past actions.* You will see how you make yourself into the failure you don't want to be. This awakening frees you from what you *thought* to be your prison of a past mistake and a self who just can't get it right.

Beyond Control

You punish yourself with distrust in what appears beyond your control. But you can give up your fright-filled struggle by treating yourself to trust. You can accept your best as enough and relax into faith right now.

However logical it might be to presume that what you cannot control may work against you, believing in that logic makes you depressed and that definitely works against you. It may seem perfectly logical to presume that you are inferior and inadequate when you do not get your way, but that vicious internal assault prevents you from getting your way.

Surrender

When controlling your life starts feeling burdensome, the time has come to surrender. Surrender the idea that tells you that you need to do more than your peace and joy and love will allow.

Just about everyone seems to blithely call life unfair. Don't they realize that affirming life's unfairness does them an injustice? Life seems unfair as long as you cheat yourself with your limited ideas of life. You give yourself the life that you think yourself in. What thoughts do you need to surrender for peace?

Affirming The Positive

Affirming everything as good, even when it hurts, can help you see the good beyond the frightening thought that binds and blinds you. Affirming that you are free, powerful, good, and magnificent when you feel down weakens self-destructive, self-berating self-assault.

When you feel worried, you might affirm, "My life always works out perfectly." When you feel like a loser, "I triumph always." When you feel undeserving, "I deserve all that I desire." Repeating this over and over can help your perception refocus on the truth of it.

The Power Of Your Subconscious

You give your subconscious direction through what you tell yourself repeatedly, especially with emotional intensity, and that forms your beliefs. Talk in pathetic voice tones about how sick you feel and you start feeling sicker. Emotionally speaking of your situation as hopeless drags you into a bleaker experience. Affirming, "I am always free to entirely succeed" helps you lose anxiety and failure.

Use positive affirmation to help you loosen your subconscious mind from negative, self-abusive beliefs. When you express negative opinions such as "this is unfair" or "this should not be happening" try saying instead, "This presents me with a golden opportunity," to help you find your miracle.

Positive affirmation helps, but it cannot undo the entire trick played on us by the mind programmed to believe in its own lies. We need more, we hunger for more, more light, more light, more light!

Conscious Thought

If I tell my child that he has disappointed me, I believe it and resent him for it. And yet, if I look honestly at my mind, I discover that I feel disappointed because of my interpretation of the event. In other words, I disappoint myself and blame that on my child.

When you stop hurting yourself you will have no one left to blame for your suffering. How can you treat you any better? Awareness functions like an invisible shield of protection against the dark power of unconscious self-mistreatment.

The real you feels loving, free, happy, and successful. The real you gratefully appreciates life's perfect present. To realize the truth of this, ask yourself how you feel about yourself right now, and watch your thinking to notice when you think yourself into a lower condition.

*"We were the shadows of a sleep,
and linked to a dreamy fancy."
- John Keats*

Key Thirteen

No matter how much you accumulate, accomplish, or win, it will never perform the magic of making you really happy.

IN FACT, THE MORE YOU COUNT on getting things, people, and accomplishments to make you happy, the more frustrated, anxious, unhappy, confused, and disgruntled you end up. Whatever you look forward to ends up disappointing you. Isn't it time that you got that?

This does not make life disappointing. It makes your abandonment of this moment disappointing. No future offers you more than all you have right now, but you deprive yourself of your present opportunity when you relate to the present as lacking in any way.

To emancipate yourself from desperation's futile pursuit, see the cost of believing that any outcome or experience offers you more than what happens right now, and that you need anything else to happen.

Growing Happy = Growing Enlightened

You don't have to get someplace else, something else, someone else to be happy; just get more aware here and now. Happiness grows with awareness. Awareness equals enlightenment. In that inner light you see the conditions that you project in your imagination as all that bring you down. Seeing how you cause your suffering empowers you to stop causing it.

The problem is that we want to be enlightened forever. But all we can be is enlightened right now. Each moment takes a new effort to pay attention, to be aware, to look within in order to see what is happening in here. We need to regenerate our light right now. Our light increases with every effort, and with it our joy. Each flash reveals a higher level of awakening to attain, a deeper dream to unweave.

The Physics Of Enlightenment

Physicists have discovered that your idea of a solid, material universe of objects outside of you, separated by space, constitutes nothing but an illusion projected by your sensory mind. Your belief in the reality of that illusion is a projection of your thinking mind. There really is no "inner" or "outer" world. There is only the world of your own consciousness.

As you raise your level of consciousness, you rise into a higher world where more love, joy, goodness, truth, and beauty prevail. To raise your level of consciousness, simply pay attention to what you are experiencing in the present and to your presumptions surrounding it.

You will then see that you *imagine* separation between you and all you desire; you *imagine* someone experiencing what you want to experience and yourself in an inferior experience; you *imagine* something lacking where you are and something better happening elsewhere. You will see that you live in an imaginary prison until you wake up to its imaginary existence.

Projecting No Choice

Sylvia believed that she had to rush all day everyday because of the brutal demands of responsible living. She told herself and everyone else that she had no choice until she believed it. Do you see how her belief in that *idea* gave her no choice? Paying closer attention to her present experience eventually revealed to her that believing in that idea was a choice, and a destructive one at that.

You Choose Your Way

Look within to see the choices that you make that incarcerate you in unhappiness. Do this when you feel tempted to look at what others do to cause your sorrow. You will see that you worry for the thrill you get from imaginary self-destruction; you lash out at those you love for the pleasure of feeling in control; you look down on others for the pleasure of feeling relatively faultless; you choose your every critical, impatient, unhappy reaction for the pleasure of fighting. You begin to see all this as you pay more attention to what you are really up to within. You feel powerless to choose a better way until you see yourself choosing your way.

Imaginary Romance

Loren felt convinced that she had met her soulmate in Tommy *soon after she married Ned.* She imagined Tommy to be superior to her husband in ways that she desired most. Paying too little attention to her mind, she unconsciously related to her *imaginary* Tommy and Ned as real people.

Loren had an affair with Tommy and eventually left Ned to be with him. In a short time she realized that Tommy was not superior at all. In fact, he seemed to become more like Ned everyday. At the same time, she began idealizing faithful old Ned.

By the time she came back to Ned to ask for one more chance, he was unavailable. Now she faced being alone, and imagined that to be her worst experience yet.

Depression And Dreaming

We imagine that we cannot feel happy, thrilled, and fulfilled until something or someone changes. We imagine that some other situation or person offers more opportunity for happiness and fulfillment. Paying attention to your mind reveals that as long as you hold onto such dreams you hold onto your depression. The source of unhappiness is unconscious imagining.

The End Of Futile Pursuit

Randy desired a woman who appeared disinterested in him. He translated her disinterest to mean his inadequacy, and that made him feel depressed. Relentlessly looking within soon revealed that he lived in this pattern in other areas by translating the lack of what he wanted into proof of his inadequacy. Any goal he had yet to achieve meant he was inadequate to achieve it.

Seeing how he imagined himself into his experience of inadequacy also revealed how doing that kept him from attaining what he desired. Recognizing its purely imaginary and presumptuous nature let him let go of that inadequate self-image, and that woman started looking his way.

Life After Death

Their marriage had had its normal problems, but after his young wife suddenly passed away Tony could not remember her or their relationship as less than perfect. His loss opened his eyes to only love.

But his bright vision turned black as he told a friend, "When you lose the best life has to offer, you only have something less to look forward to. My future looks like death from here."

"Look at your experience of death," his friend suggested. "Just face it. Look at it until you see its source within you."

Tony lived with his inner death for years. Examining it gave him no quick fix. Only the strength of character to endure, with the grace of God, got him through. Then one spring morning he noticed that he felt delight with the newness of life.

Do You Want To Be Close Or Closed In?

Brandon felt thrilled upon entering a new relationship but the woman soon found his demanding neediness unbearable. He thought he just wanted to be close, but to her it felt like he was constantly closing in. Finally she could take no more of it and ended their fresh affair.

Without her now, Brandon decided to face his pain instead of seeking someone else to ease it. He passed through an excruciating period of almost unbearable anxiety. He came to discover deep down inside that he desired the inner strength to live courageously on his own more than he wanted a mate. In time he got both.

How We Separate Ourselves From What We Desire

When you experience a division between you and what you desire, *you separate yourself from what you desire.* To release yourself from separation to real fulfillment look at your thoughts when you feel a desire. Based on appearances, you imagine that what you desire is separate from you, that your present circumstances are lacking in comparison with the circumstances you desire. You project yourself out of fulfillment, into loss and lack.

To Receive Your Miracle Now

Try this exercise to enter the miracle you desire now. Describe in writing one life-condition that you deeply desire. Now, what makes you *think* that you are not presently *in* that condition? In what way is your life different from that condition? If you pay close attention to your thinking and remain strictly honest with yourself, you have to admit that you *imagine* yourself in or out of that condition.

Be on the lookout for any thinking going on in you that places you outside of the conditions you want to live in. It's fine if you can imagine yourself in the conditions you want, because you bring about what you think about. But to experience real freedom, the freedom of your miraculous existence, you simply need to see the purely imaginary nature of your separation from whatever it is you desire to experience.

When you stop telling yourself that what you want is *not* happening, you then begin experiencing all you want. Bring this exercise into your daily life. Be on the inner lookout (the vigilant look*in*) to notice when you *imagine* separation from what you want and *imagine* what you have as inferior by comparison. This ends depression.

Consumed By Imagination

To experience anger, fear, or discouragement you have to imagine yourself into some dismal condition and relate to that imaginary condition as your reality. You either expect what you do not want or you interpret what is happening in some way that bothers you. In both instances, your imagination consumes you.

Instead of focusing on what you are depressed about, focus on the experience of depression itself. Look *within* to see what makes it happen. When you feel frustrated, anxious, or unhappy ask yourself, "What am I projecting within?" Then look within. Soon you will see that your mind is playing a tragic movie that is eating you up, and you will let that movie starve to death.

Disappointment Deceives

You experience disappointment when you interpret an outcome as a loss. In other words, that which disappoints you exists nowhere but in your imagination. That imaginary scenario covers the total opportunity that is present, and so you bring about the loss that you imagine. The fact is, though, that every situation can work for you miraculously. Holding onto imaginary loss prevents you from recognizing your gain. Disappointment deceives you into believing in its possibility, while nothing will ever take your miracle from you.

The Art Of Conscious Projection

You begin feeling unhappy, forlorn, displaced by life when you project an imaginary condition that does not work for you. When you get all caught up in daily life's "outer" affairs, you overlook the projecting going on in you and think yourself into problems that you can't seem to escape. Becoming aware of this projecting dispels your depressing sense of powerlessness and releases your power to intentionally shape your destiny.

Think about what you want to happen. Then, stay conscious to recognize when you project the occurrence of what you want to avoid. Spend some time intentionally thinking about what you want and be on the alert to recognize when you think about what you do not want to bring about. This is the art of conscious projection. It gives you your power to design your destiny.

Life presents you with the opportunity to create the life you want. The problems that you project within form your experiences of living without. You unconsciously choose a life you don't want. Choose to direct attention within to enter the life you want.

Streams Of Light

As you awaken to your inner life, you begin to sense streams of darkness and streams of light. The streams of dark flow through your dismal imaginary projections. As you consciously view the dark streams you get into the streams of light. The light leads you on the path of delight. It reveals the inner vision of your faith and your heavenly connection.

When you feel let down you have left the light stream and entered the dark stream. You have begun unconsciously living in a dark projection. Higher guidance flows to you in the stream of light as you bring the light of more conscious attention to your struggle.

We Use Ideas As Maps

In yet another Bob Dylan song, we hear the phrase, "using ideas as maps." Take a look at your idea-maps. You have a map of me in your head. You have a map of yourself. You have a map of your life. The map may point the way to trouble and despair. The map may portray a territory that depresses you with heavy care.

You discover the reality of the road, though, only when you lay down your map and pay attention to what is actually going on where you are. Can you see the difference?

"The map is not the territory."
-Count Alfred Korzybski

Key Fourteen

Seeing the illusory nature of the notion
that you have too much to overcome
is a major breakthrough.

JOHN BELIEVED THAT too much darkness engulfed his spirit to ever make it into the light. When he examined this dismal condition, he saw it was just a dark movie of the mind and realized, laughing, that light had made it in.

Unconscious mental imagery tyrannizes us like spells cast by a hidden, ruthless wizard. Looking within shines the light of revelation through the halls of mind, exposing the sham of the dark, truth-concealing tyrant. This elevates us above unconscious mind's dark power to defeat us, where we find ourselves basking in the happy light of freedom.

Abandon Your Abandoned "Self"

Alexander angrily complained to his wife about how she made him feel unloved, unappreciated, unimportant. After catching on to what you are learning here, she gently urged him to look within to find the real cause of his suffering. He went off by himself and paid attention to his thoughts. He soon discovered that he fought for and against false selves.

He fought *for* a mental mirage of himself feeling rejected, uncared for, love-starved. He fought *against* a mental mirage of his wife expressing indifference. All at once he saw the futility of trying to change the condition that he held onto.

When You Resent Someone

When you resent someone look within and you will see a mental image of a victim with which you identify as yourself, and a mental image of a villain with which you identify as the other. Your resentment feeds on the unjust scene that you hold in your mind until you see how *you give yourself* that abusive treatment by holding onto that scene.

No adversary is any more powerful than your thought of that adversary's power. You are only as powerless as you think you are. Imagine yourself being infinitely capable. Then stay clear of any thought of being any less.

No Predicament Has Power Over You

You *are* all the power you need. When you feel overpowered, you expect too little of yourself. You imagine yourself right out of power and freedom. No situation denies you of opportunity. When you cannot win one way, you can win another.

All that happens offers you all the help you need to succeed. This you clearly see when you let go of the idea of any obstacle you face as too great. You always have the power to design, determine, and enter the great destiny you desire.

Imaginary Plights

If you feel unloved, you imagine yourself in that condition. If you feel unsuccessful, blocked, limited in any way, you imagine yourself in that plight. Instead of wishing and waiting for your life to change, let go of the mental movie plots that that you do not want to live in.

Paul regretted his past, believing that it set him up for future failure. He had done things that he wished he hadn't, and that led him to feel undeserving of success. His sense of loss and disappointment seemed inescapable.

His spirits began to rise as he realized that the self he saw in his mind, and the past choices of that self that haunted him, were really just flashing forms of mind. He affirmed to himself repeatedly, "I am not my thought of me" and this helped him release the internal activity that made his past his problem. He soon saw those mental movies of past mistakes differently, as positive motivators to live now with integrity.

To Be A Better Person

Tricia wanted to be a better person. She wanted to express more talent in her art. She wanted to be more skilled in the business side of her work. She wanted to treat the people closest to her with more kindness. But as much as she wanted this, she seemed to become no better.

"I feel trapped in who I am," she shared with a caring friend. The friend suggested, "Before you try to improve yourself, wouldn't it be wise to first discover yourself?"

"But I know who I am," Tricia argued. "I know who I want to be."

"Look again," said her friend. "See the person you think you are. See your image in your mental mirror. Continue looking at it until you realize that you are the viewer of that image, not the image."

Tricia practiced this and saw how she imposed the limits upon herself that she longed to leave.

How To Unlearn Unhappy Patterns

The child adopts the patterns to which he is repeatedly exposed. Similar to the way that your father became angry, you become angry. Similar to the way that your mother became depressed, you become depressed. This represents one way that you learned the self-defeating patterns that undermine your happiness.

One important step toward unlearning your unhappy patterns consists in identifying the individual who modeled them for you. Look at the ways that you make yourself miserable and ask yourself, "Who in my past does that remind me of?" As you begin to recognize the person who gave you the pattern, you may find yourself feeling trapped, imprisoned, captured by that person's influence.

Continue looking at what is going on in your mind and you will see that to be a false scenario that you need not accept.

Where Are You Bound?

We imagine what we fear and we live in the experience that we imagine ourselves in. If you worry about being bound for conditions that will not support you, you imagine yourself right out of that support now. Imagine the bottom dropping out from under you, imagine yourself surrounded by stupid, worthless people, imagine yourself a stupid, worthless person and that becomes your world. You are bound *in* the experience that you imagine.

Abusing Power

In Vail's childhood someone abused his position of power over her. In her adulthood, Vail feared that anyone she counted on would do the same. She routinely saw herself in a dependent, vulnerable position and felt entrapped by it. Her voice would quiver with a pathetic, placating tone when she spoke with her employer. She habitually hunched her shoulders to look small, obsequious, and servile when her mother-in-law entered her kitchen. She loathed herself for being an impotent, cowardly sycophant.

Then, in other instances, Vail would switch roles and become the power-abuser. When someone made a mistake in her eyes, her rage over being taken advantage of might explode without warning into a merciless, vicious verbal attack. This pattern left one relationship after another in ruins and she loathed herself for cruelty and its costs.

Looking within led her to the realization of how she abused herself with her power of thought. She *envisioned* each scene of her past and present victimization. She *envisioned* the victim and the villain roles she played. Her higher level of consciousness overcame the power of abuse.

Powerful Illusions

Waking up to how you handle your own power hands you all the power you need. It ends the powerful illusions that any condition can dominate you. When you feel powerless to alter or overcome a condition, you are merely *imagining* yourself in that condition. A problem or a person dominates you only as long as you imagine yourself inferior and dependent.

Worry about what a situation or a person will do to you and you make that situation or that person in charge. Your humiliating sense of dependency begins in your imagination and ends in awareness of what your imagination is up to. Any time you feel intimidated, overpowered, or overwhelmed, instead of looking at how a situation or person has power over you, look within to see how you use your power. As you see how you handle your power, you find yourself less concerned with how others handle theirs.

The Failure To Control

The more frustrated you feel in a relationship, the more you waste your effort trying to make the other person change. The idea that you need the other to be different in any way is all that keeps you from finding happiness. When you let go of that idea you can stop seeking happiness in a way guaranteed to keep you unhappy.

Look back at times when you desperately struggled for control to see:

- *You felt miserable while you acted that way.*
- *Your attempt to control was based on an imaginary need to control.*
- *You resented that other person for "making" you work so hard at controlling him or her.*
- *Your stressful attempt to control resulted in your frustrating, even maddening sense of futility.*
- *You blamed your painful control-pattern on the person you presumed needed your control.*

What's In Charge?

When we experience the deepest sense of loss, we imagine that we abide in an existence without order. View such experiences without drawing any arbitrary conclusions and they transform into a field of unlimited possibility that places *you* in charge.

When you achieve what you set out to achieve, you believe in order. When you try and fail, you lose faith in that belief. But if you continue relying on law and order, you find that works. Your destiny follows the path of your intention, supported by consistent action, guided by intelligence and love, aimed at the accomplishment of your goals.

Imagine nothing less than perfect, divine, loving order in charge of what happens to you.

Beneath Complaint

Blaming and complaining generate more of the conditions that we blame and complain about. While complaining about how unhelpful her family was, Dawn observed that the more she complained, the more helpless and dependent she felt and the more unfair and inconsiderate her family seemed. She looked within and saw how she habitually imagined things going wrong in her life and then looked for someone to blame and complain about. The practice of paying attention to her inner life released Dawn's power to steer clear of the idea that she needed anything more from others than they willingly offered.

We Live In A Cyclical Universe

Just like recurring seasons in nature, the "seasons" of our lives return cyclically. For instance, you face similar challenges with your mate today that you faced with your parents in childhood. You find yourself attempting to hide your rebellious behaviors from your child today somewhat similarly to the ways that you tried to hide them from your parents. Your child makes you deal with at least some of what you made your parents deal with.

The symbol of life is the spinning wheel. You cannot stop the spinning as long as you live, *but you can raise it to a higher level.*

By paying close attention to how you create what happens, you see how to transform past tragedies into present triumphs and past triumphs into downright miracles.

The Point

Have you ever felt so disenchanted by life that you wondered, "What's the point?" When you count on something you want to happen to you, you miss the point of what happens. Instead of judging or resisting whatever occurs, *look at what you make of it.* That is the one and only way to stop making it into what you do not want.

This present moment is nothing more or less than your way of living it. Do you feel unhappy, unsuccessful, undeserving? Do you feel blocked or let down? Just look at how you create that experience to find yourself beyond its boundaries.

What do you imagine keeping you from feeling totally happy, in love, fulfilled, successful, and worthwhile right now?

The unwatched imagination locks you into so-called "misfortune." The observed imagination presents you with the key of liberation.

"Nothing routes us
but the villainy of our fears."
-William Shakespeare

Key Fifteen

Relate with your emotional reactions as experiences to explore.

EMOTIONAL REACTIONS cloud perception. Under the influence of an angry, unhappy, insecure feeling you confuse your mind's action upon you with some other cause. You believe, for instance, that another person has to change for you to feel better, while only your thought of that person disturbs you. Imagine trying to repair your car by working on your house! This compares to the effort to end self-caused misery by trying to cause someone else to function differently. It must lead only to a sense of increasing frustration and futility.

To see the confusing influence of emotion, and to release yourself from that confusion at the same time, instead of looking *from* your emotional condition, look *at* it.

A Valuable Lesson

Hank felt down when customers he had trusted with credit did not follow through on their promise to pay. "I can't trust anyone," he bemoaned. "Not even myself anymore. How could I have been so stupid!"

Then he learned to look *at* his feelings rather than *from* them and something wonderful happened. He saw the mental images that kept him emotionally down, including visions of himself as inadequate and of his life devoid of prosperity. He saw further that dwelling in these hopeless fantasies left him too demoralized to work with his full capacity for the life he really wanted. In other words, his dark mental visions were functioning as self-fulfilling prophecies!

Seeing this lifted his spirits instantly. Instead of imagining the kinds of customers he did not want, he imagined the ones he wanted. Instead of beating himself up for what he had allowed to occur, he thought about the future he wanted and focused on taking steps to reach it, including a slight shift in his business practice to prevent a similar kind of loss.

But Hank felt most thrilled by the realization that looking *at* his emotional condition revealed and cleared the confusion that produced it, similar to the way that morning sun evaporates foggy mist.

Return To Peaceful Power

Patiently viewing any unhappy emotional condition gradually clarifies the false version of reality playing like a movie in your head that causes it. This returns you to your natural state of peaceful power where you find yourself free to think about what you want - instead of what you fear - which leads you into actions that manifest the fulfillment of your desires.

Disturbing Emotional Reactions Command You

Disturbing emotional reactions command you to create imaginary situations that fuel them. The stronger the emotion, the more vivid the vision it fabricates until you feel absolutely convinced that you are reacting to a situation over which you have no control.

Seething with feelings of frustration, Stephanie imagined her son wasting the little time she had to work, thereby determining an unsuccessful future for her. Looking *at* her angry emotional defeat revealed the purely imaginary nature of the situation she wanted out of, and that released her from it.

Emotions Use Power

Emotional reactions run on your energy. That is why an intense, angry reaction leaves you feeling worn out after the charge of it wears off. You lose energy, or power, to all forms of emotional negativity that you engage in, including jealousy, anxiety, discouragement, impatience, and rage. The stronger the reaction, the more depleted it leaves you.

When you view your experience of an emotional reaction you release the energy locked up in the emotion. It flows into your awareness, awakening you to new insight. You can then see how to fulfill your purposes.

The Inner Critic

Sandra had been raised by an extremely critical mother who routinely complained about her life and the people in it. Sandra, in her own adulthood, carried within her that same inner critic that defined her home, her job, her vacations, her possessions, her marriage, even her children, as lacking. This made her feel even more frustrated by the constant urge to escape the inescapable. She felt so disturbed that she quickly, easily, and frequently flew into a rage over the slightest deviation from her expectations.

When she was finally ready to give up trying to find satisfaction through criticism, she sought freedom by observing her critical reactions. The amount of pain she felt surprised her. Soon, she discovered that the pain increased the more she thought about what bothered her. Continuing to examine her experience of critical feelings gradually released her from their grip as she realized, "I am being critical because I am *choosing* the critical state, not because of who or what I criticize."

Hear Your Voice

Pay close attention to the sound of your voice. You may be stunned to hear how frequently and how vehemently you complain, criticize, condescend, and condemn. Listen to how much annoyance and arrogance you express in your tone of voice. Speaking in these modes talks you into an unappreciative, ungrateful, unforgiving, and unhappy point of view.

The Life You Make For Yourself

Observe how your angry, critical reactions make you feel, speak, think, and act and look at the consequences of that. You will see that all you create under their influence are circumstances to feel even unhappier about. You make yourself a life you don't want as long as your disturbing emotional reactions remain your unexamined responses to circumstances. Your way out of that life begins as you direct your attention into a conscious examination of your inner experience. You will quickly see that you actually resent nothing but an imaginary condition you have been unconsciously placing yourself in.

Who Do Your Reactions Turn You Into?

Amy lost her temper over her husband's apparent oblivion of their young child's public display of embarrassing behavior. She held it in until she found a place where she could privately explode in a verbal assault. As she began with, "How could you be so irresponsible..." she happened to glance at a reflection of herself in a nearby mirror.

This reminded her to apply the lesson you are learning here. She stopped talking, excused herself, and walked off on her own to focus full attention on the experience of her wrath. This required that she live in her pain and look at it instead of seeking freedom by dumping it on him.

She observed: "I get so caught up in trying to change my husband that I overlook what I am making of myself." She did not want to be the person who related in that severe manner to her husband and finally came to see that he did not make her into that.

Looking Out A Dirty Window

Looking outside through a dirty window, you might imagine a gloomy gray day and feel depressed about the weather. Shift from looking through the window to looking at it and you see that the pane of glass needs cleaning.

Looking at your life through disappointed or disapproving emotional perspectives makes your life seem dismal. Then you live in a sense of futility and blame it on a power beyond your control. Living in a defeated, angry attitude repels people who view life from a more victorious perspective. It also attracts to you other disgruntled people who reinforce your beliefs in defeat.

Set Unhappy People Free

Unhappy people sink into the murky waters of their muddled mind. The drag of their descent will pull you down, you will slip under the influence of the dark spell they cast upon themselves, if you do not carefully watch your own mind closely in their presence.

You cannot make others happy as long as they insist on keeping themselves miserable. Trying too hard to lighten up another can cost you the energy you need to maintain your own light. The purpose of an encounter with an unhappy person is to help you to recognize the negativity in you.

Say "Goodbye" To Darkness

See how you feel about and think about others. A critical, condescending, condemning attitude toward someone you see as too critical, condescending, and condemning expresses your own dark perspective. Your negativity can only abide in the darkness of unconsciousness. Shining the light of awareness onto your inner self sheds you of your emotional darkness like rising dawn sheds night.

Try this exercise to say "Goodbye" to darkness. Think of a person you feel critical toward. It doesn't even have to be anyone you know personally. Perhaps you dislike someone you hear on the radio or see on TV. Next, ask yourself, "Where does this person exist?" To be honest with yourself, you have to admit that this "person" exists in your mind as a mental image that triggers your resentment.

Now look at your feelings in response to this mental image. Simply examine them without resistance as they abide in you. Gradually, you will see that there really is no reason to hold onto this negativity and you'll find peaceful release.

You Can Never "Fix" Yourself

You can never "fix" yourself through self-criticism, because criticizing yourself means that you identify with a mental image of a self you believe needs fixing. Becoming all you want to be occurs as you see the confusion at the root of all unforgiveness: unconsciously identifying with a mental image of a self.

No one can free you from the ways you make yourself unhappy. You have to see for yourself how you disturb yourself. If you ask me, "Okay, I believe you, so what can I do to stop upsetting myself?" you miss the point. You *automatically stop hurting yourself when you see how you hurt yourself.* Your simple solution is to continue looking until you find freedom.

Open Pandora's Box

Remember the myth of Pandora's box? That box contained all the evils of the world. By opening the box Pandora released those evils. The box symbolizes your unconscious. Open it by prying into it with your awareness and you release a seemingly unlimited store of anger, fear, resentment, bitterness, depression, shame, jealousy, feelings of inadequacy and even hatred. You free yourself from emotional darkness by looking within until you see its methods of existence.

Freedom Beyond Control

Until you look at what you are really looking at, people and circumstances beyond your control seem to cause your problems, disappointments, and frustrations. You cause yourself to feel jealous, inadequate, wrong, and even doomed. Blame, criticism, complaining, and condemnation attach you to your injuries. Freedom awaits your discovery that every depressing view of your life, of yourself, of other people is nothing but a mental projection that you unconsciously enter and live in.

When you encounter the limits of your power a Greater Power has taken charge, never a lesser power. You are never trapped by circumstances beyond your control. Rather, you are always set free by them. You do not have to control what you cannot control because everything is already under perfect control, too perfect for you to imagine.

Every event to which you fearfully react offers you a key to how you produce, and how to release yourself from, the unhappy reactions that keep you from all you want in life. But you must take the key in hand and put it to good use.

" . . . We form our judgment, ordinarily, not on the evidence of life itself but on those quite different images which preserve nothing of life. . . ."
-Marcel Proust

Key Sixteen

When you feel threatened or defeated you've slipped into a dream.

YOU MANIFEST what you imagine. You receive all that you are willing to accept. Imagine no limits and accept the miraculous!

Pay alert attention to your mental activity and you can avoid a descent into the dark world of lack, limitation, and loss. Is your life less than the life you desire? See the *imaginary* condition of your inadequate life. Directly face your life as it is to find its total fullness.

Seek to consciously awaken to your deepest, truest, ultimate desire. That lets your desire define your destiny. Even though you cannot articulate what you ultimately want, your attention directed toward it directs your life toward it because...

Your Life Follows The Direction Of Your Attention.

Dan imagined that he led a blander life than some of his friends, because they traveled far more than he did. He just could not come up with a way to make it happen within his means, and he couldn't seem to increase his means sufficiently. He resented himself for not measuring up.

Then Dan stood watch over his mind until he saw his thoughts defining his life and himself as lacking. When he entered his present experience with full attention, without troubling himself by mentally comparing, he found himself utterly free of his problem.

What you imagine ripens on the tree of your life until it comes to fruition in the form of your experience. You nurture your vision by living in it as if it is your reality. You manifest loss by imagining loss. To enter the life you want, direct your attention into the life you have.

Beyond Desire

Examine what seems to separate you from what you desire and you enter the life you desire, because what you desire most is truth. When you imagine what you want as a condition that differs from your present experience, you live in an imaginary state of separation from what you want. Seeing this starts setting you free.

All you want waits for you beyond your imaginary barrier to it. Life impels you to continue reaching upward, to reach for what you imagine being beyond you. When you see the boundary as imaginary, it begins to melt. Then you are ready to let go of striving and enjoy arriving.

All limits upon your fulfillment are entirely imaginary. The walls that keep you bound from fulfillment disintegrate as you simply see them clearly. The instant that you experience a desire, you draw to you the experience you desire. Nothing but illusion produces the absence of what you want.

Cheated?

When you pine over a loss, carry a grudge, look fretfully into your future, look down on yourself or on someone else, you give yourself an experience that you don't want to live in. You can do this only without realizing it.

The fear wrought by the illusion of lack poisons your well of infinite abundance. The habitual feeling of deprivation feeds off of your fantasies of someone else having what you wish you had. You feel betrayed by the life you unconsciously choose, because unconsciousness is designed to betray you. You *choose* to feel cheated and to believe that you need more from life and from other people. This drives you into conflict, unhappiness, resentment, and regret.

When you imagine that someone treats you unfairly, *you imagine it.* You give yourself the unfair treatment by occupying your mind with the notion of it.

Consciousness Is All You Need

To the extent that you suffer with any sense of lack in your life, *you manifest the lack you loathe.* How? By unconsciously imagining your experience of it. If you were to imagine it consciously, you would stop, because you would *see* yourself taking yourself out of freedom and abundance by doing so.

As you pay more attention to your inner life you see yourself depriving yourself of the miracle that you desire *right before you stop doing that.*

View your thinking until you see that you *think* you are going through what you think. Then you will see that when you think of yourself as a victim, you become your own victimizer.

From Anger To Forgiveness

Barry told his friend about the magnificent, palatial home of a client of his. Looking within as he spoke, Barry noticed that:

- *He felt deprived, imagining that he lived in an inferior home and therefore an inferior life.*
- *He felt depressed about this.*
- *He resented himself for not being able to afford an equal or superior home.*
- *He tried to think of something about his client to criticize to camouflage his painful sense of inadequacy.*

Upon noticing all of this, Barry said to himself, "Why give myself all of this pain in response to a gorgeous home?" Realizing how he punished himself freed him.

Living In Lies

Those who hold onto their illusions look in vain for real fulfillment. Living a lie can never truly satisfy. It is, in fact, the root cause of dissatisfaction.

You live in a lie when you play the role of a victim, because you imagine less than all you desire coming your way. You live in a lie when you act as though *anyone* has in any way diminished your unlimited worth and opportunity here and now. You live in a lie when you insist that you need others to do something for you that they resist doing.

When You Don't Get Your Way

Observe what happens when you do not get your way. You merely presume that you are not getting your way because you want things to appear differently, and that prevents you from living in the greater good that is possible. Then you feel you have less.

When you want something else to be happening, you place yourself in an imaginary experience of something going wrong.

Why People Blame
You do not blame because of what happens to you. You blame because you are asleep. The more you blame, the more wrong you feel. We blame for four reasons:
- *We know of no better way to feel free (of responsibility).*
- *We do not observe the results of blame.*
- *We do not recognize the illusory basis of blame.*
- *Blaming has become a habitual reaction when conditions don't match our expectations.*

The "Those-Were-The-Days" Daze
Like you, I was raised in a culture that disparaged loss as inferior to gain. Because you lose with every breath you exhale, this value-system drives one to fearfully resist and angrily condemn the inevitable. It also locks you into the illusion that receiving the experience of loss is not a gain of infinite blessing, and that what is actually happening cannot be infinitely superior to the way that you imagine it to be.

Every loss sets you free to receive something greater. Letting go of all you don't want is the price you have to pay for all you do want. Resisting loss increases its cost. Face loss as a natural cycle of living. Consciously examining your experience of loss teaches you how illusory loss really is. When you curse a loss you reject the greater gift that it offers to you.

Nostalgically looking back to better times costs you the rich fulfillment now offered to you. Your history is a dream, and dreams are meant for deliberately defining your future. Loss leaves when you let go of the past.

Light Dissolves Despair

The light of awareness, as has been stressed here, functions like sunlight. As the light of the sun dissolves a vaporous cloud, so does your beam of awareness dissolve the clouds of sorrow and despair. A steady focus of awareness directed onto how you are feeling turns your feeling into joy.

Fran's husband left her with their two young children for another woman. Fran learned from a mutual friend that her ex and his new mate recently returned from a Caribbean cruise. Another friend reported that he saw them zipping around town in a snazzy new sports car. Fran felt taken advantage of. She imagined that no one would want her in her situation, imagined that she had been thrown into an inferior life, and that seemed so unfair. She felt angry, depressed and used condemnation of *him* as a shield against facing the failure that she imagined herself to be.

Her unhappiness troubled her children and their attitude, grades and behavior all suffered. It took intentional looking within, facing her most unpleasant feelings, including her utterly agonizing feelings of envy and worthlessness and a lonely future, for Fran to recognize that her mind delivered her betrayal. By relentlessly looking at the broken hearted beliefs and emotions she only wanted to avoid, her path to freedom cleared.

Be For You

Looking within reveals your world of hurt to be rooted in the imaginary. What happens is totally *for* you. Opposing life's changes pits you against your own interests. When you drop the idea that you do not have what you want, you see that you can have it.

Abandon Defeat

Any feeling that you experience is worth looking into. Looking into your feeling of defeat, for instance, discloses how absolutely unfounded it is.

The wise know that so-called "defeat" offers you the opportunity to prepare yourself to achieve greater victories. When you do not get your way, consider the changes you need to make for your way.

Consciously sinking into disappointment shows you how to rise above it in the future. Loss offers lessons in how to lose and how to win, a wisdom that can lift you higher in every way.

Freedom From Unhappiness

Just because you felt disappointed, anxious, or angry a moment ago does not mean that you have to lug that condition with you into the now. Stop remembering how you feel. Enter *this* instant with full attention to *this* instant to find your instant freedom.

You feel unhappy when you project a disappointing vision of your life. Instead of looking at your future through your mind, look at your mind as it projects your future now. Then you can leave your disappointing future behind.

Knots Of Time

One of the greatest Romantic poets, William Wordsworth, invented a concept that he termed "spots of time." These "spots" consist of luminous memories that light us up with rapture when our minds return to them. We also have what I call "knots of time". These consist of dark, painful memories that we seem inextricably bound to.

Toni felt trapped in a knot of time, reliving in her mind

over and over the giving up of her baby for adoption. Mitch felt tied to the day he came home from work to find that his wife had left him and taken their infant son with her.

Every time you return to one of your "time knots" you hurt yourself all over again. To untie your "time knots," look within until you see that it is not the past, but a present imaginary projection that ties you now in painful emotional knots. This permits a present of release to become one of your new luminous spots of time.

*"It's all just a dream, a vacuous scheme
that sucks you into feeling like this."*
-Bob Dylan

Key Seventeen

Through every turn of events you find that you really can count on life.

YOU FEEL SO NERVOUS because you unconsciously presume that you have to control more than you can. You do not escape feelings of insecurity by reacting in a panic. All you have to deal with, when you feel insecure, is your state of insecurity. By directing the light of awareness into your feeling of insecurity you turn into peace.

See how you *think* your way into insecurity. You imagine your life falling short of your needs. Then you fear you have too much to control.

Right State
An experienced race car driver knows that looking at the wall as you speed around a curve draws you toward that wall.

Your life's direction functions similarly. Worrying about frightening possibilities draws you into them because *what you imagine forms the shape of things to come.*

Your emotional state attunes you to the thought-dreams you receive. A frightened state imagines disaster. An angry state conceives of injustice. A feeling of confidence brings visions of victory.

To utilize the divine creative power of human thought, it behooves you to enter what we can term the *Right State* for thinking. Right State is the inner condition of peace, security, and inspiration that attunes your mind to your most sacred dreams.

To Overcome Anxiety

When you feel anxious or insecure, look at how you feel. Your feelings of insecurity attract a vision that feeds them. To overcome this:

- *See where the condition you keep actually exists: nowhere but in your mind.*
- *See it for what it is: nothing but a thought.*
- *Then focus your attention on your feelings. Just feel how you heal for awhile.*
- *Now think about the success you had feared your adversity might take from you.*

When any disturbing thought occurs, instantly let it go by refocusing on your feelings—without the thought that feeds them.

Advancing to Adversity

The appearance of adversity signals your progress, not your regress. It means that you have graduated to another challenge. Every setback offers you a step up into higher accomplishment. Obstacles, losses, dangers, and letdowns mean it's time to grow into your greater potential. Encountering frustrating limits points your way into infinity.

To Live In Your Miracle

Tommy believed that he felt depressed because he was stuck with a bickering mate. But he wondered why at other times he felt totally blessed to be in his marriage. When he looked within he saw that it had to do with the feeling state he thought from. First, he saw that his nightmare marriage existed nowhere but in thought. Then he saw that when he felt good inside, he saw his marriage as his miracle.

"To live in your miracle," he later divulged, "think only from love."

Joanne felt defeated by her habit of yelling at those she loved. When she observed her thinking and its relationship to her feelings she saw that she *imagined* this defeat when she felt powerless and depressed.

Perhaps you imagine yourself with no way out of a dead-end job or a strapped financial condition or a flat life. You live in the misery of these imaginary conditions as long as you imagine yourself in them. And you imagine yourself in them as long as you imagine your life *from* feelings of defeat.

Defeating Images

You cannot defeat an image. You imagine someone overpowering you in a discussion and no matter how many times you revisit that image you always come out a loser. Look at your feelings when you feel defeated until you see that you do not have to choose to live in that state. Outside of the feeling of defeat the image of defeat remains at bay.

Imagine yourself watching a movie of yourself failing at a particular endeavor. Each time that you fail in the movie, you identify with that imaginary failure and suffer its sense of defeat. You watch this movie over and over again in the futile hope of seeing the movie turn out differently. *But you produce that movie,* so you end up feeling beaten by it over and over and over again.

Your imagination is not a window to the past, present, or future. It is a mental movie. You are drawn into the movie that your feelings attune you to.

How To Stop Fighting A Losing Battle

Watch your feelings. As soon as your feelings plummet, you enter a mental movie of your undoing. If you can remain alert enough, when you feel any trace of inner discord you can focus your attention fully on your feelings and avoid thinking yourself into a condition that reinforces your unhappiness.

It helps me to keep from thinking by focusing on the physical sensations of my breathing. I observe the present sensation of the air making contact with my nose or mouth, my chest expanding and contracting. This helps me to avoid thinking from a state that attracts misfortune.

If you must think, then think your thoughts consciously. Say to each disturbing thought, "You are just a thought." When I do that it takes me out of that thought.

Recognize your imaginary losing battles as nothing but mental creations. Then you can drop them and feel like a winner again.

How We Do Unto Others

We treat others poorly when we feel poorly treated. But the poor treatment you experience, you give to yourself. The pressure you place on yourself, which you cannot stand, you place on others. You cannot set yourself free and you cannot let others be until you learn how to lighten up on yourself.

You over-burden yourself with the presumption that you have to do more, be more, control more to be safe enough to feel happy. But to feel happy, you need only to cease imagining limitations.

When You React From Unhappiness

When you react from unhappiness you fight against an imaginary villain, for an imaginary victim, both of which your unhappiness produces. And the more energy you put into the fight, the more defeated you end up feeling.

Haven't you noticed that when you angrily attack another, if he remains unmoved, you feel worse? Why is that? Because you have demonstrated no control over what you frightfully believe you need to control. That person has forced you to face your issue with control. If you don't face it, your rage can build to a maddening degree. If you do face it, you soon find yourself released. In a sense, that other person shared his release with you.

What Do You Think About Life?

Nature shows us how to live in the joy of life. The bird enjoys free flight. The fish enjoys swimming free in the ocean. If you do not enjoy your freedom to live this moment your way, you falsely imagine yourself not free to do so.

When you think of a situation you enter the thought of it as reality for as long as that thought lasts. Imagine yourself in a condition that you want to experience and you enter that condition in your mind.

Thought, then, is an illusion that you enter. It seems real as long as you live in it. What is the life you think yourself in?

Any Thought That Freezes You In Fear

Any thought that freezes you in fear is a thought attracted by fear. You already live in the life that you anticipate. When you feel happy, in love, secure you anticipate success.

It is not unusual to feel some resistance toward your greatest dreams coming true. At least your disappointment feels familiar and it matches who you think you are. You want to live in your comfort zone, with all of its discomforts. All that stands between you and any level or form of success that you desire is your fear of success. You are afraid to lose yourself. You do not want to die. You have to release your known life to enter another form of life.

Here is how to make that journey to success. Stop thinking from *Wrong State*. Wrong State is a state in which you feel the pressure to control more than you can. Don't brace yourself for anything. Let yourself *feel* free. Then you *are* free.

Your Great Destiny

Your great destiny comes your way as you set yourself free in the present. The more you push for what you want, the more you pressure yourself and others for it, the more you push it away.

To achieve all the success that you truly desire, feel your way into the freedom of this moment. Stay aware of your feelings to let go of forcing, pushing or struggling to make something happen or to resist something happening. Feeling free melts the barriers of perception standing between you and your miracle.

Anger Reinforces Fear

Fear underlies anger. When you react in anger, you draw upon anger to compensate for your fear of lost control. Your anger only ends up fueling your fear, though, because it drives you into destructive actions that produce more havoc out of your circumstances. In other words, angry reactions create circumstances that spin even more out of your control.

When you feel angry, you make yourself angry by entering the angry state to hide your fear. If you pay closer attention to how you feel, you see how to move from fear to faith.

Every once in a while an angry flare up may give you the spark of energy you need to make a breakthrough. But this is extremely rare. You rarely benefit by living in an angry spirit.

Look at what you feel angry about and you see a condition generated by the frightened state of your own mind. Feeling angry about your life means that you have gotten too locked into your belief in a loss.

Living With The Enemy

In order to feel angry with someone, your mind creates a mental scene of that person behaving in a way that makes you feel taken advantage of, overpowered, and out of control. You keep company with that overbearing psychic entity as long as you imagine yourself in that scene. Obviously, as long as you blame the actual person for the angry way you think of him there is no real escape.

Remember the last time that you felt annoyed with someone? You probably did not look at your mind to see yourself reacting to your mental creation.

The Source Of Painful Memory

The source of painful memories is not painful past events, but an inharmonious feeling state that tunes you into them in the present.

Kimberly felt hurt after her sister spoke to her in a condescending tone at a party the night before. The episode churned in her memory all day, distracting her from her work. She brought it to bed with her and it kept her up at night. The next morning, she spoke about it with her husband. She felt so annoyed that the conversation quickly turned into a spat.

Finally she broke her chain of thought by focusing her attention on her feelings in the present instead of on her memory. She soon noticed that she felt good inside, and the painful memory could not attack her.

The Source Of Negative Speech

The next time that you hear someone expressing a negative point of view, turning the topic of conversation into problems, losses, mishaps, notice the physical signs of how that person feels. You will see that she speaks from troubled feelings, and that permits her to see only trouble. Understanding this will help you to avoid taking her criticisms and complaints too seriously.

To help her, don't argue against her negative perspective and don't agree with it. Relate with her *feelings*. Treating her kindly, patiently, and from a good, harmonious feeling state yourself may help her to feel better, which in turn will raise her perspective to a higher world, where she can begin thinking and speaking about what she really wants to bring about.

Dreaming And Destiny

When you think about yourself, another person, your past, your future, or the way things are, you view a condition of imaginary substance, what Shakespeare described as "The stuff that dreams are made of." Dreams are powerful in at least two ways:
- *You live in the dream as reality as long as the dream lasts.*
- *The dreams you dwell in are harbingers of things to come.*

Your feelings draw your dreams to you, and your dreams draw your destiny. The dreams feelings draw feed the feelings that attract them. To leave a troubled life, let go of troubling dreams. Step one is to see each dream as a dream. Then, to ward off troubling dreams, remain aware of how you feel until you feel trouble free.

"Those who do not observe the movements of their own minds must of necessity be unhappy."
-Marcus Aurelius

Key Eighteen

You cannot think a worthwhile thought outside of a harmonious feeling state.

READ THIS BOOK ONE HUNDRED times to offset the life-long barrage of cultural programming that has been hypnotizing you to confuse your disturbing ideas with reality, that has been programming you to blame the world for the hell-of-a-world you mentally create for yourself.

How you feel determines what you think and what you think designs your world. Think from anger and receive only visions that fuel your anger and keep you trapped in the world you desperately seek flight from.

See Your Thoughts

See your thoughts as just your thoughts. See your feelings as the magnetic field that brings your thoughts to mind. You receive thoughts in harmony with your feelings.

If your life depresses you, pay closer attention to your mind until you see that only your thoughts of life depress you. And why do you receive such thoughts? Because you think from a depressing feeling state.

Your Natural Feeling State

We can describe the right feeling state for thinking as the feeling state that allows you to see life through the vision of faith, with a heart filled with love and inspiration. We can call this your *Natural Feeling State* because you don't have to *make* yourself feel that way. You *naturally* feel that way because *life* is love inspired. You can see only beautiful perspectives, possibilities, and solutions on the wings of thought that come to you from your Natural Feeling State.

To Leave A Disappointing Situation

To leave a disappointing situation leave the angry, insecure, unhappy feeling that brings the idea of it to mind. To accomplish this, look at your mind until you see the thought that feeds your disturbed feeling as nothing but a thought. Then focus on your feelings, not on the thought, until awareness returns you to your Natural Feeling State.

Unhappiness Is A Way Of Life

You are happy or unhappy according to the way you live. Paying close attention to how you live reveals that you are free to choose an enjoyable, loving way to go about things by functioning in your Natural Feeling State.

Happiness is another word for your Natural Feeling State. It makes you powerful, peaceful, positive, healthy, beautiful, creative, intelligent, appreciative, loving, forgiving, attractive and in harmony with your highest aspirations and delight.

Living outside of your Natural Feeling State means that you are unhappy, which makes you less effective in every way but the ways that hurt. You feel overpowered, negative, unhealthy, ugly, uncreative, ungrateful, unloved, unforgiving, and you attract people and circumstances that supply you with every reason to feel that way.

Without A Disturbing Thought

Your feelings return to their natural state of harmony in the absence of a disturbing thought. Your Natural Feeling State then brings you beautiful, loving, forgiving, inspiring perspectives that translate into loving, forgiving, and inspiring treatment from other people and the marvelous circumstances that make your miracle reality.

No Time To Think

There is a time to think and a time to not think. To know if it is the right time to think, look at the quality of your thoughts. Do you see people hurting you? Do you see yourself hurting others? Do you see yourself stuck? Do you see an ugly scene? Do you see something going wrong? Regard such disturbed thinking as your cue to switch from thinking to a conscious focus of attention on your feelings until you find your way back into your Natural Feeling State.

You Are As Unsuccessful As You Think You Are

Do you see your life as a total success, or do you see something missing? If you see anything lacking, you manifest that lack through your thought of it. If you still believe your life is the way you think of it, continue looking at your thought of your life until you see that as erroneous.

If you cannot see yourself in the condition you want to be in you are thinking from an inharmonious feeling state. Unconscious thinking from a state of inharmonious feeling turns your mind into your prison.

You Are All You Want To Be

When you see your life as lacking, you feel a lack of respect for yourself. You think at the time that you need to change your life to feel better about yourself, but that never seems to work because your negative self-view prevents you from creating the conditions in life that you desire.

You draw to your mind perspectives or mental versions of yourself that feed the feeling state that draws them. To liberate your magnificence, drop the ideas that portray you as less than all you could ever hope or want to be. If you have difficulty doing this:

- *Pay closer attention to your thoughts of yourself until you see them as nothing but thoughts.*
- *Then pay attention to your feelings, without thinking, to find your way back to the inner harmony of your Natural Feeling State.*
- *To determine if you feel good enough to enter the world of thought again, look at the next thought that arises.*
- *If it portrays you or your life in a less than beautiful, inspiring form, repeat the above three steps.*

A Formula For Doomed Relationships

Who do you think you are in a relationship with? If you see your mate as less than your totally beautiful, brilliant blessing your perspective degrades your relationship. That perspective can only spring from an inharmonious feeling state.

If you feel less than honored to be with your mate, your

dark feelings darken your thoughts, and your dark thoughts darken your married life. If you feel less than totally grateful for your relationship, you *think* yourself into a relationship you do not appreciate.

For The Relationship Your Heart Desires

For the relationship your heart desires engage in no thought about your mate or your relationship that makes you feel less than fulfilled. If your thought of your mate dampens your inspiration, you think of him or her at the wrong time. You do not resent your mate for letting you down. You resent the image of your mate letting you down that your mind, tainted by a wounded feeling, delivers to you. Seeing this sets you free. To enter the relationship your heart desires view your relationship only from your Natural Feeling State.

Facing Emptiness

I felt as though I had lost too much to want any more. It seemed that all my past disappointments suddenly snowballed into one totally demolishing avalanche of fortune's reversal. I felt like a hollowed man just going through the motions of living, motions without meaning. I had crash-landed on the hard, hard ground of disillusionment.

After working through my deepest sorrow in the way you are learning in this book to work through yours, I began running into individuals going through a similar form of existential crisis. "It's funny," I thought, "how I encounter those who seem to need what I now have to offer." I think that all I went through was for you, as much as it was for me.

Just when you think it is time to give up on life, it is actually time to give up on your *thoughts* about your life. You feel like a failure because you identify with the image of a failure that you view in your head. You worry because you imagine that everything may not be under perfect control. Life appears to conflict with your desires because you imagine yourself in a no-win situation.

When you hit bottom, you actually have reason to celebrate. By releasing yourself from your fear at this deep level you release your faith at this level, which unlimits your life's happy outcome.

Enter Life's Emptiness

Many of us, perhaps the vast majority, would prefer to run from the inevitable bout with the emptiness of life lived unconsciously in thought.

Try instead to face your pain until you see that what you imagine going wrong really can be going perfectly right. Awaken from the dream of life's emptiness by seeing it as nothing more than the product of your emotional mode of imaginary projection.

Breathe It In, Breathe It Out

You hold onto life's emptiness by holding onto your ideas of its emptiness, by holding onto your emotional feeling of life's wrongness. The simple act of breathing demonstrates higher wisdom. Notice what happens after you exhale all the way. You naturally inhale. If you resist, you can keep the air out of your lungs a little longer, but that requires unnatural effort.

Your life works exactly like that. Every loss precedes a gain. Emptiness turns into a new state of fullness.

When your thoughts bring you down, focus on your feelings to let them go. Your mind empties itself of negativity this way. When you reestablish yourself in your natural state of feeling in harmony again, you will receive new, bright visions like a fresh breath of air filling your lungs with new life.

Take Charge Of Your Dreams

You take charge of your life when you take charge of your dreams. The first step requires looking squarely at your depressing, frightening, frustrating notions and visions. Stress, anxiety and depression depart as you see that nothing but a dream justifies them.

Look in your heart and accept what you desire. Think about what you want and drop any idea of it as absent. If you have no idea of what you want, drop the idea that tells you that you need to know. If you can't imagine yourself in a better situation, if you find it hard to accept a better situation, let yourself feel good without a thought right now.

Envisioning what you want works, but we push for it too hard when we disparage what we have, when we demean whatever is. Nothing can make you happier, more fulfilled or more secure than your release from the internal habit-reactions that make you unhappy now.

You Are Now

You are not the person you were; you are the person imagining that person.

Happy Coincidence

When you predict your greatest dreams coming true and release imagined scenarios portraying anything less than that, life meets your faith with success via happy coincidence.

Your Imaginary Life

On the negative side, your imagination has caused *all* your feelings of depression, anger, fear, stress, insecurity, and dependency, making you less effective in achieving the circumstances that you have wanted. The positive power of your imaginary life has been demonstrated by the number of times you have brought about the desired conditions you first thought about.

Sleep Enough To Wake Up

I recently felt worried about a situation. I noticed that I felt tired as well. Understanding that a tired state acts like a conductor to worrisome thinking, I laid down and looked within. Almost instantly I fell asleep. When I awoke, just a few minutes later, my worry had gone. The lesson: rest enough to awaken from dreams of your undoing.

The Myth Of Money

People lie, steal and cheat for money based on the absurd expectation that they can find true happiness from such underhanded, selfish conduct. People give up on the dream of what they really want to do with their lives, based on the mere belief that they must sacrifice a decent life to make a decent living.

Standards

Do you think that your life has to look a certain way for you to deserve respect? The way your life looks is the way that you envision it. If your vision costs you self-respect, drop it.

Do you think you have to live up to someone's standards to respect yourself? The life you compare to any standards exists solely in your mind. When you see your life below a standard you lose your power to raise your life to a higher level.

Grief

Face your grief until you see it's caused by a dream to awaken to the miracle of limitless life.

"Now I find hidden away in my nature
something that tells me that nothing in the whole
world is meaningless, and suffering least of all."
- Oscar Wilde

Part 2

Majestic Indolence

18 Light Supports

THE TITLE OF THIS BOOK says it all: Lighten Up! By that I mean for you to let light *in* to your heart and mind, the light of clear awareness; also, to let your lightness be, the lightness of release from dark, heavy brooding. To truly lighten up involves so much more than just, "Don't sweat the small stuff." It's not that simplistic. You first have to see what makes you feel so small and what makes the "stuff" of life look too big and too heavy for you to handle. You have to wake up to how your mind works for you and how it works against you to finally see how life, with all of its twists and turns, its beginnings and endings, its up and its downs is truly for you, never against you.

Lightening up requires some basic daily practices as foundation work. These provide the inner strength to support the "altitude" of awareness needed to see beyond the illusions of fear. Apply them gently, lightly, expanding your application of them by small, unstrained degrees.

1. Lightening up begins with directing the beam of your attention within to light up your thoughts and feelings, to simply be more conscious of your inner life.
2. Notice what you talk yourself into when you speak, and what you allow others to talk you into when you listen.
3. When you feel the strain of anxiety, frustration, or discouragement setting in, trust easing up on yourself instead of merely wishing life could be easier.

4. Take all the rest you need. Fatigue fuels receptivity to negativity. Sometimes, it takes nothing more than a brief nap to dispose of nagging despair.

5. Keep your days 98% free of rush. Trying to do too quickly, speak too quickly, or even figure things out and decide too quickly creates conflict and rejects joyful success.

6. Practice "listening" to your inner sense of what you need to do to feel balanced, in harmony, content in the now. Driving yourself too hard drives good fortune away. Whatever you lose your balance for, you lose.

7. Eat light. Stuffing oneself with rich, heavy food past the point of fullness lowers vitality, making living burdensome.

8. Work out physically. Regular physical exercise invigorates the body, clarifies the mind, and discharges destructive stress.

9. Embrace opportunities for solitude. Until you learn how to be alone you make too many demands on others. In solitude you can get to know yourself better and discover better ways of treating yourself.

10. Pursue the fulfillment of your higher potential. Drop the idea that you must decline with age. Aim at getting better every year.

11. Reject false obligations. Making yourself miserable for another's happiness never works because when you feel miserable you cannot resist making everyone around you feel just as badly. You are the instrument through which you function; taking excellent care of yourself fulfills your first responsibility.

12. When you feel out of control, trust that a greater power is perfectly in control.

13. Practice doing whatever must be done (what you choose to do) in a way that you enjoy.

14. Relate to each event life brings as an opportunity to learn

how to live through it.

15. When you feel worried about what may occur, remember that for all you know everything is working out fine; trust in the basic goodness of whatever is.

16. Give yourself a lift by doing what you love.

17. Attract the best people by giving your best to the people around you.

18. Practice the miraculous Creative Law of 7: Spend 7 minutes a day writing down 7 conditions that you would love to occur in your life within the next 7 years. By the end of 7 years, most if not all of those wonderful dreams will have come true.

"The time has now arrived at which they must raise the eye of the soul to the universal light which lightens all things, and behold the absolute good."

—Plato

Majestic Indolence

"MAJESTIC INDOLENCE" is another one of those phrases coined by Wordsworth, like the poet's *"Spots of time"* discussed earlier in this book. It refers to a relaxing contemplation of the good, the true, the beautiful that uplifts the soul. It conveys the essence of lightening up.

An example of Majestic Indolence might be to take a break from a chore to spend a few moments "idly" gazing at the clouds in appreciation of their collosal magnificence. The grandeur that you receive through your eyes enters you in spirit, nurturing *your* collosal magnificence.

Another example might be picking up a guitar, even if you don't know how to play, to "idly" strum for attunement to your inspiration. Reading this book would be a form of Majestic Indolence for you if you don't work too hard at making sense of its lines, but rather allow its light to lift you without strain.

In the above paragraphs I have placed the word "idle" in quotation marks because the apparent display of idleness may prove profoundly productive.

Light Work

Majestic Indolence serves a critical role in our best work. A recent study found that giving a 100% effort to a task actually diminishes one's effectiveness. Apply yourself more casually to your work, taking no aspect of it too seriously, even maintaining a somewhat playful attitude, and you perform at your highest level, produce your best results. In other words lightening up is a key to raising the level of your performance.

Majestic Indolence constitutes a key component to the wise way to pass through life's tough tests and trials. Within each moment exists a center of delight. If you are gentle enough on yourself, you open yourself to that core and receive enough of its lift to get you through with faith.

Easing Yourself Through Experience

Easing yourself through experience nurtures your joy, inspiration and love. Abandon the pressure that robs you of the ability to delight in life, that drives you into depression. You do not demonstrate irresponsibility by allowing yourself the luxurious, pure pleasure of connecting with the splendor of God's creation, you beautify the light you bring to the world.

The sublime exists here, now for those who have the courage and the faith to allow life's goodness to enter them. You either imprison yourself or you *"imparadise"* yourself in this moment, depending upon how you choose to live it.

No One Steals Majestic Indolence From You

Others can make demands upon you, but what you choose to do about those demands is always entirely up to you. The habit of hurry, worry and grim seriousness drives you out of the healthy, happy, restorative splendor of Majestic Indolence.

Parents complain that their child makes them yell. Spouses complain that their spouse makes them argue. Employees complain that their boss makes them work too hard and too long. Employers complain that they have to work too hard to keep their employees from slacking off. All of these are lies. You work too hard because you either do not trust, or do not value enough, your ever-present freedom to center yourself in the sacred present.

Though you may feel that you do not have time for Majestic Indolence, the time you have loses its value when you sacrifice Majestic Indolence for slavish industry.

To realize the work of grace in your life, live gracefully. Majestic Indolence attunes you to the love of God's Mercy. With its peaceful power of joy you can receive the miraculous life-changes you desire.

How To Practice Majestic Indolence

Stop *doing* too much and let yourself *be*. Just be. Just being is a sheer delight. It feeds your soul with the lightness of being.

You say you have too many problems, too much responsibility for Majestic Indolence? Majestic Indolence has, throughout the ages, been a central aspect of the way of work for our greatest achievers. Ask the masters of any field and they will tell you that they make sure to relax enough to have fun with what they do. Enslaving yourself to a task makes it meaningless and renders your best results no better than bland. Those who take things too seriously are driving themselves mad.

By gently looking into your inner life with openness and wonder, you practice Majestic Indolence and your consciousness rises to heavenly planes.

Majestic Solutions

Your solutions do not come from worry. Worry fills the mind with darkness, leaving no room for light. Whatever you worry about worsens because worry wears you out, making you less capable. It also focuses your mind on what you do not want, and you bring about what you think about.

To make the right decision every time, don't worry about which decision is right and which is wrong. Instead, focus on *how* you decide. Decide in the right way. The right way to come to a decision is with inner peace, faith, and clarity. If you work too hard to get it right you sacrifice those internal conditions.

Majestic Indolence takes you beyond misfortune, because whatever is going on, you can find the peace of inspiration you need to rise above it.

A marriage falls apart when the couple works too hard at the business of controlling one another, failing to let go and trust enough to sufficiently enjoy just *being* with each other. If your marriage is currently in trouble, try this solution: stop trying so hard to change or control your mate. Practice the self-discipline of letting things be enough for Majestic Indolence to soften your heart.

You make your problems too big to solve when you work too hard to solve them.

Majestic Upliftment

Let Majestic Indolence free you from the habit of living in overdrive. Apply the self-discipline necessary to work with focused relaxation and attention without tension.

Majestic Indolence is not to be confused with sloth or slovenliness. One can be indolent without being majestic. The majestic nature of your indolence depends upon how you indulge in your freedom. Make your indolence majestic by opening your heart to love and inspiration.

Have Faith In The Impossible

Without faith in the impossible you work too hard, believing you have to make everything happen through extreme effort. But without faith in grace, the faith you demonstrate through Majestic Indolence, all joy, all meaning, and the best work you can do is lost.

It is impossible that Milton wrote *Paradise Lost*, that anyone could have used language as masterfully as Shakespeare, that the teachings of Jesus could be so deep and true, that the Bible's Psalms could convey such wisdom and demonstrate such divine eloquence, that Buddha's teachings could show the workings of the mind so clearly, that Beethoven and Mozart could harvest such momentous sounds from silence, that Michelangelo, Raphael, Leonardo da Vinci, the ancient Greek architects, and countless others could manifest such physical beauty through their work. But these miracles occurred. They blossomed from hearts and minds that took the time to be still enough to let beauty fill their souls with rapture.

Do the same and you join their miraculous ranks. Harness the power of happiness in Majestic Indolence to create your beautiful destiny!

"He was too indolent in the happy languor
of the moment to answer the question."
-Joseph Conrad

Enlightening Affirmations

Use the following affirmations as little light-thoughts to give your consciousness a slight lift. Repeat each one 18 times in a row, in a state of relaxed openness.

"I am clearly aware of the inner cause of how I feel."

"I let go of imaginary difficulties."

"I trust the Greater Power that is in control."

"I choose to live my way."

"I choose to take excellent care of myself."

"I trust my enjoyable, natural, unstrained ease."

"I trust the way that all is."

"I release myself from imaginary scenes of someone hurting me."

"I release myself from imaginary scenes of me hurting others."

"I have all the power I need to accomplish all I want."

"Easing up enough to enjoy my life now brings me my great good fortune."

"I release imaginary limitations and accept the limitless now."

"I see failure as entirely imaginary."

"Seeing time-limits as nothing but a thought frees me from the notion of having too little time."

"I am not who I think I am, but the thinker of that thought."

"I am free to live the life I want to live right now."

"I look at life through the eyes of faith."

"I am naturally at peace."

"He spake, and into every heart his words
carried new strength and courage"
–Homer

Luminations

Read one of these light aphorisms a day for the next 18 days to spark your remembrance of the light.

What you think about you bring about.

When we imagine a wasted life we waste our life believing in the waste that we imagine.

To lighten up, simply notice the dark weight of your mind's depressing illusions.

Holding onto the thought of yourself feeling unhappy makes you unhappy.

Your challenges call upon your greater potential.

Holding onto ideas of what is going on, of who you are, of who the people in your life are, blocks the birth of your greater understanding.

Consciously descend to bottom of your grief to reach the pinnacle of fearless joy.

You have to stop imagining yourself let down to realize how life is offering you a way up.

Recognize the illusory nature of your mind's limiting projections to enjoy unlimited freedom.

For all you really know, the miracle you want your life to be is happening now.

Holding onto ideas of injustice is all that keeps forgiveness from you.

See how nothing but your thinking delivers depression, resentment, failure, and loss.

Suffering arrives to purify, strengthen and expand your acceptance of love.

When you imagine someone looking down on you, you belittle yourself.

You are either humble or humiliated. Take nothing personally. Let go of every insult or you insult yourself. Let go of praise or lose your authenticity.

The better you treat yourself, the less you have to resent others for their treatment of you.

When struggle begins, take a vacation from struggle.

Nothing comes to an end as long as you are, except in your head.

"All sciences and arts are directed in an orderly way toward one thing, that is, to the perfection of man which is his happiness."
-St. Thomas Aquinas

Light Exercises

The following exercises are designed to strengthen your inner light. You might choose to do 1 a day as an 18-day program.

-1-

Take a long, slow, calming breath. Relax your body and
affirm the following:
I consciously observe my mind's activities.
Then spend as much time as is comfortable doing that.

-2-

Take a long, slow, calming breath. Relax your body and
affirm the following:
I consciously observe my feelings.
Then spend as much time as is comfortable doing that.

-3-

Write down a brief statement describing a condition that you
would like to happen in your life. Then, notice how you feel.
If you feel any trace of discouragement or uncertainty about it
taking place affirm:
*For all I know there is absolutely no reason
to feel discouraged about this.*

-*4*-

Take a long, slow, calming breath. Relax your body and affirm the
following:
My past exists in thought alone. My future is a present thought.
Then spend as long as you like paying attention to your thoughts.
When you notice a thought of any past or future condition or event,
say to it:
You are just a thought.

-*5*-

Write a brief statement describing something that is lacking in
your life. It could be a sum of money. It could be a home. It
could be a person. It could even be a talent you would like to
express. Then take a long, slow, calming breath. Relax your body
and affirm the following:
I release myself from the condition of lack by not imagining it.

-*6*-

Write a brief statement describing a possibility that you would
love to be happening in your life now. Then take a long, slow,
calming breath. Relax your body and watch your mind, being
on the lookout to notice any thought that portrays your life
without that condition. When you notice such a thought, state:
I do not need to live in joy-negating thought.

-7-

Whatever you feel desperate for retreats, because desperation means you live in the idea of being kept from what you feel desperate for. If there is any condition or person that you feel desperate for, affirm:

I release myself from desperation as I accept
that nothing stands in the way of my fulfillment.

-8-

Who have you left to forgive? Think of one individual that you feel angry, resentful, critical, annoyed, or anything less than loving toward. Then, look at your feelings toward that person and state aloud:

The treatment I received from others exists
nowhere but in my thought of it now.

-9-

When you are conscious enough in the present, you see that your thought of a person or condition is just a thought, which empowers you to let go of problems instead of holding onto them. You see that how you feel is a state you place yourself in, which empowers you to let inharmonious feelings go. To help you to be more aware of your present experience, focus attention on your breathing. Spend as much time as you like with your attention fixed on the flow of air as you inhale and exhale. Notice the present sensation of your breath, without thinking of the sensation you just had. When your mind drifts, bring it back to this focus.

-10-

If you had endless time, what three conditions would you accept as possible for you. Write those down. Then affirm:
All time limits are imaginary.

-11-

Think of a person that you find difficult to get along with. See that person in your mind, and affirm:
The person that I see in thought is a figment of my imagination.

-12-

If you recalled only the good others did you, how would you feel about your life and the people you have known? Let yourself feel feel for the next few minutes the good others have done you. And let yourself think about that for a while. Then affirm:
I always find the good I seek.

-13-

Bring to mind something you did, or left undone, in your past that you regret. What are the consequences of it that you fear? Write down your answers. Then affirm:
For all I know this can cost me nothing.

-14-

What condition in your life do you feel the most impatient to change? Write that down, then affirm:
When I stop imagining any time at all between where I am and want to be, my detainment ceases to be.

-15-

What skill, power, or ability can you think of which, if you had more of, you could accomplish more of what you want to accomplish? Write down your answer. Then affirm:
I lose the limitations that I do not imagine.

-16-

Think of a situation in which you felt taken advantage of or disgraced. See the scene in your mind. Then remind yourself:
I live in the world I think myself into.
I give to myself the experience that I think of.

-17-

Think of someone from your past who mocked you, criticized you, or put you down with enough severity to hurt your feelings and wound your self-image, so that you find it more difficult to completely believe in yourself to this day. Then affirm:
I need not define myself through anyone else's eyes.

-18-

Think of a miracle you would love to happen Then state:
For all I know, in my world no miracle is impossible.

"...my vision, being purified,
was piercing more and more within the rays
of light sublime, which in itself is true."
-Dante

Songs Of Light

-1-

When it all falls apart,
another dream breaks your heart.
when counting on another promise gleaming
leaves you leaning into careening;
when you've taken one more risk,
puckered up for one more kiss,
dipped your hand into the pot
to give more than you thought you got,
and in one more ending you begin,
from one more loss go for your win,
to end up tumbling into a lonesome spin;
when another broken hope hobbles by
and you dig in deep to climb or crawl that stony steep,
your eyes cast high toward the very peak,
and your foot-stone dislodges,
like some vanishing mirage is,
and you hear someone laughing -
see the joke on yourself played
by nothing but a mental shade.

- 2 -

When you think you're running late
you hurry and you worry -
when you drop that thought you enter
the present right on time;
when you think you cannot make it,
to give up, you cannot take it -
when you drop that thought you enter
the power to go on;
when you criticize and complain
you feel let down and drained -
when you drop thought's wrongs you enter
the way that all is right;
when you think your lost in darkness
and struggle vainly against the night -
when you drop that thought you enter
the long embrace of limitless light

- 3 -

All is a movement
onward and upward
a triumph of the will;
you cannot lose
whatever you choose
great purpose you fulfill;
so hail the fading of the day
greet the dawn with cheer
only in the dreams of thought
exist the scenes your fear has wrought
the good is here
for vision clear
a triumph of the will.

- 4 -

Lose worry about your future -
it's groundless, you always land on your feet;
and depression over the goal you've yet to capture -
the game's not over, you're not beat;
cling not to what you've got
nor grab at what is not -
both materialize thought of loss;
nor fear by fault you're failure-caught
you've erred before and found
another hope's rebound;
envision dreams you want to come true -
you'll find life's rhyme as they manifest for you.

- 5 -

When Delays Frighten You
all that keeps you from delight
is the idea of you in a pitiful plight;
when this you do finally see
from fear's snare-mind you're finally free;
the worries that you propagate
mis-shape your destiny -
in faith's vision form your fate
and all you want will not be late.

- 6 -

What you imagine happening to you
is a mental movie seeming real;
watch your thoughts to know that's true
and happy freedom you will feel;
all you have without dark thought
is nothing but bright blessings,
every wound that loss has brought
delivers love's caressings;
whatever you worry about is not—
be here now without thought;
nothing at all is going wrong
in the light where you belong.

- 7 -

When trouble hits,
* ask yourself, "what can i learn from this?*
what can i gain, even from the pain?"
then listen with your inner ear
to the words of wisdom ringing clear,
"i can learn how to love and let go
and how to win and lose;
i can learn how to go with life's flow
when i get what i would never choose;
i can build up my faith in life
and believe in something higher,
and in the midst of strife
toward deeper peace aspire;
i can think back to how i made this,
learn my lesson, see my blunder, move on,
and master the art of forgiveness

a little kinder to become;
i can learn how to live a little better
without fear's futile defense;"
thus i from myself unfetter
the troubling fantasy i'm dead-set against.

- 8 -

Two paths to joy are chosen
only one leads not astray;
exit the night-mind frozen,
enter bright new day.
one struggles to acquire
and preserve it all from loss
joins the club of liars
pretends to be the boss;
the other seeks release from
what shatters joy right now:
just empty, sad illusion -
awareness shows him how;
to lose it all, to win it all,
to the second both the same -
doorways to the inner hall
of light's palace of the unslaved;
within both have the power
but only one has found the key
to unlock miracle's shower
and ascend to pure beauty;
all you desire is your condition
when you drop fear's imaginary vision;
freedom has no division,
your miracle no intermission.

- 9 -

Dismal reflections about me hovered;
thick, dark, heavy cloudlike they covered
my early mind, held captive in a shadowy ring
awaiting light's awakening
to see from a new mind at last
the spell that thought upon me cast,
that i am not a victim caught,
just asleep in a nightmare's plot:
blocked, undeserving, lost,
a self bound to a self self-crossed;
that was the life i accepted for free
until i saw as fantasy
those dismal thoughts depriving me
 of true light's bright awakening.

- 10 -

Desperation burns as you yearn
but it pushes the sought for away;
what you want so much you beg for
leaves you and that is for sure
as farther from truth do you stray
till emptied by your hunger for more
you finally descend into your core;
now you're ready to stand on your own
when what you sought comes to your home:
the fruit of the freedom you have sown.

- 11 -

You fight against your fate
imagining a life you hate;
to lose this spell of living hell
learn the wisdom of living well:
imagining your life unblessed
makes you feel that you're oppressed;
you squirm and writhe inside your mind
as it conceives of your tight bind;
thinking of yourself as stuck
makes you feel so out of luck -
drop the notion of now as less
than all you wish for happiness.

- 12 -

Let dark fears pass and the shadows they cast
of cold sorrows go, then you'll know:
let what is be; do not believe
it must be bad 'cause you feel sad;
let life do what life does;
loss just frees you from what was;
imagining crisis makes heads spin,
to be free, just look within;
life by law must compensate,
each dark night has its bright mate;
now is how you're loved by fate,
never a moment to berate.

- 13 -

When you've slid down life's slippery slope
with barely a reason left for hope
and doom you fearfully resist
in a frightening illusion you exist;
to wake up from your sad dream
chant with heart the following:
a greater power takes care of me
in a way I may not see
i have faith when all seems lost
i have faith love's worth the cost
i have faith in life's changes
i have faith despite the dangers
i have faith all can be won
i have faith in what is done
i have faith life works somehow
i have faith in faith right now

- 14 -

What am I projecting
causing me my stress?
i'm being taken advantage of,
i'm left with having less;
what am i projecting
that I feel so down?
that guy is setting me up,
i'm nothing but a clown;
what am i projecting
causing me to fight?
that guy is out to get me,
he just gave me a slight;

what am i projecting
that's disappointing me?
dead, bland, flat results,
in a poor destiny;
what am i projecting
that makes life feel so rough?
i cannot trust my natural ease,
i'm just not good enough;
what am i projecting
that i feel so not-free?
i'm all walled in with no way out,
this is no place for me;
what am i projecting
that i feel so off-track?
my life is stuck on empty
and all i have is lack;
what am i projecting
that i feel so insecure?
i do not have what it takes,
and i deserve loss for sure;
and when i'm done projecting
through awareness of my mind
i exit sad confusion
and depart from fear's grim bind.

- 15 -
When you receive the miracle you pray for
but by the time it finally arrives
you feel too emotionally beaten
to fully appreciate the surprise,
examine your inner experience;
you'll see how you hold on
to the death of dead-inspiration
and its view of life's value gone;
in that momentous moment
you'll realize with wonder-filled eyes
the greater light around your life
which really is the prize.

- 16 -
There's nothing but love
and it carries you through
into the miracle that proves it's true;
all arrives for your release
from imaginary shackles for freedom's increase;
you can trust both day and night,
you only lose in thoughts' dim light;
in the limitless you stand -
mere ideas degrade a life so grand;
greet the now without a thought
to disprove the loveless lie thought brought.

- 17 -

You cannot feel depressed
without imagining you're oppressed
then in sad dream you're born,
where you lost and feel forlorn;
imagining you're in where you want out
keeps you where you think about;
you think of lack and it makes you sore;
you think of your life as broken and poor;
your sorry lot comes down to this:
your thought encloses you in a tragic myth;
see this and you are set free
to happily soar into infinity.

- 18 -

I drop all thought that tells me all is not
all I want to be
then all i want belongs to me
and i belong to being free
no limit have i, none
as new as now
as wise as always
i am everywhere unbound
god awakening
the undefined
the unconfined
self of
laughing
horizonless
deathless
light

"We must eradicate from the soul all fear and terror of what comes out of the future ... And we must think only that whatever comes is given us by inner world direction, full of wisdom."
-Rudolf Steiner

The Beginning

BOB LANCER

Bob Lancer has been inspiring, enlightening, liberating and empowering audiences with his fresh approach to wisdom for over 25 years through his books, recordings, inspiring keynotes and dynamic seminars. He leads listeners around the world to their next level through his radio show that has been on the air since 1995 and broadcasts to 35 states over the radio, and worldwide over the internet. He is a devoted parent, husband and canine companion currently residing in Atlanta, Georgia.

BOB LANCER'S
Inspiring *Lighten Up!* Keynotes and Seminars
Banish Doubt and Deliver Hope

Bob Lancer inspires and empowers audiences around the world with his profound message of hope and possibility so needed at this time.

Invite Bob Lancer to *lighten up* your company, school, place of worship or association.

Visit:
BobLancer.com

➡ To schedule or learn more about a *Lighten Up!* speaking engagement, seminar, or teleseminar

➡ To see a complete list of Bob Lancer's books, recordings and videos

➡ For Bob Lancer's bio and other pertinent information for meeting planners and media

Bob Lancer's Radio Show

Presenting Timeless Wisdom
For 21st Century Life, Work,
Relationship and Parenting Solutions

Lightening Up Listeners On WSB Radio Since 1995

Stations, Times & Websites

Newstalk 750 AM
Late Night Sundays:12:30 AM E.S.T. (Technically Monday Morning)
Broadcasts throughout the state of Georgia and the surrounding 35
states.Streaming worldwide simultaneously over the Internet on
www.wsbradio.com

97.1 FM (The River)
Sunday Mornings: 6:30 AM E.S.T. Broadcasts throughout Greater
Metro Atlanta, GA. Streaming worldwide simultaneously over the
Internet on **www.971theriver.com**

B98.5 FM
Sunday Mornings, airing 2 shows back-to-back: 4:30 AM–5:30 AM
E.S.T. Broadcasts throughout Greater Metro Atlanta, GA. Streaming
worldwide simultaneously over the Internet on **www.b98.com**

ADDITIONAL TITLES BY BOB LANCER

Available at boblancer.com

PARENTING WITH LOVE, WITHOUT ANGER OR STRESS:

Discover a new way to parent. Learn how to raise your child by raising your level of consciousness. Discover how to parent in peace and poise, with your heart centered in love, as you meet the challenges of child behavior. End draining power-struggles. Learn how to fulfill your parental responsibilities without sacrificing the sacred joy of parenting. Relate with your child in the deeply loving, conscious way that protects and preserves the sacred joy of childhood, even as you prepare your child for a conscious, responsible life.

THE SOULMATE PROCESS:

You can manifest just about any condition you choose, but doing so involves a conscious cooperation with certain natural and spiritual laws. This book reveals those laws and provides practices for working within them to manifest the love of your life. Read touching examples and learn how to apply simple principles and practices to find the person right for you or to recharge your existing relationship with the miracle of "soulmate energy."

KABBALAH CARDS:

Use this simple method based on the ancient Kabbalah Tree of Life to tap higher levels of creativity and intuition to help you find your way to any goals.

THE LONGTIME TALES OF UNCLE MO

A book to motivate children to achieve their dreams with compassion. Bob Lanceris illustrated childrenís book of humorous, motivational tales for children ages 3–12. Assists in character development and fosters reading skills, language appreciation and creative thought. Includes pictures children can color. Read about the first Popsicle Wedding, a dog named Sit and the septuagenarian who wins rodeos!

Bob Lancer's Inspiring Audio CDS
(Each approximately 50 minutes in length)

For ordering information, and to see a more complete list of books, CD's and videos, as well as an abundance of free Lancer's Answers to guide you on your way, go to:

www.BobLancer.com

How (and Why) to Be Grateful for Everything/ How (and Why) to Forgive Everyone (Including Yourself!)

What to Do About Your Thinking!

Why Everything Happens to You (and What to Do About it)

Exit Mind Havoc

End Depression Now

Your Victorious Self

Balanced Living / Naturally Succeeding

Overcoming Loss and Finding Inspiration

Empowerment and Peace Through Meditation

Inevitable Success

Exit Anger

The Power of Patience

Encountering Powerlessness